Mike Holt's

LEADERSHIP SKILLS
TAKING YOUR CAREER TO THE NEXT LEVEL

Mike Holt Enterprises
888.NEC.CODE (632.2633) • www.MikeHolt.com

NOTICE TO THE READER

The publisher does not warrant or guarantee any of the products described herein or perform any independent analysis in connection with any of the product information contained herein. The publisher does not assume, and expressly disclaims, any obligation to obtain and include information other than that provided to it by the manufacturer.

The reader is expressly warned to consider and adopt all safety precautions that might be indicated by the activities herein and to avoid all potential hazards. By following the instructions contained herein, the reader willingly assumes all risks in connection with such instructions.

The publisher makes no representation or warranties of any kind, including but not limited to, the warranties of fitness for particular purpose or merchantability, nor are any such representations implied with respect to the material set forth herein, and the publisher takes no responsibility with respect to such material. The publisher shall not be liable for any special, consequential, or exemplary damages resulting, in whole or part, from the reader's use of, or reliance upon, this material.

Mike Holt's Leadership Skills— Taking Your Career to the Next Level
Third Printing: June 2023

Author: Mike Holt
Layout Design and Typesetting: Cathleen Kwas

COPYRIGHT © 2016 Charles Michael Holt

Produced and Printed in the USA

All rights reserved. No part of this work covered by the copyright hereon may be reproduced or used in any form or by any means graphic, electronic, or mechanical, including photocopying, recording, taping, or information storage and retrieval systems without the written permission of the publisher. You can request permission to use material from this text by e-mailing Info@MikeHolt.com.

For more information, call 888.NEC.CODE (632.2633), or e-mail Info@MikeHolt.com.

 This logo is a registered trademark of Mike Holt Enterprises, Inc.

If you are an instructor and would like to request an examination copy of this or other Mike Holt Publications:

Call: 888.NEC.CODE (632.2633) • Fax: 352.360.0983
E-mail: Info@MikeHolt.com • Visit: www.MikeHolt.com/Instructors

You can download a sample PDF of all our publications
by visiting www.MikeHolt.com.

I dedicate this book to the
Lord Jesus Christ, *my mentor and teacher.*
Proverbs 16:3

TABLE OF CONTENTS

ABOUT THE AUTHOR vi

PREFACE vii

INTRODUCTION 1

SECTION 1—PERSONAL BRANDING 3
Appearance 4
Attitude 6
Conduct 8
Confidence 9
Reputation 11

SECTION 2—DEVELOPING BASIC SKILLS 13
Communication 14
Goal-Setting 17
"No"—the Most Difficult Word 21
Organization 22
Planning 23
Relating to Your Customers 25
Teamwork 27
Time Management 28

SECTION 3—RAISING YOUR GAME 33
80:20 Rule – The Pareto Principle 34
Assuming Responsibility 36
Creativity 39
Decision-Making 40
Managing Your Money 43
Methods of Learning 44
Mistakes 45
Peer Pressure 47
Problem Solving 48
Weaknesses 50

SECTION 4—DEVELOPING OTHERS 53
Choosing Your Management Style 54
Delegation 56
Instilling confidence in others 59
Management by Crisis 60
Motivation 61

SECTION 5—STAYING ON TOP OF YOUR GAME 65
Burnout 66
Change 69
Continuous Education 71
Memberships 74
Procrastination 75
Stress Management 77

FINAL THOUGHTS 81
Summary of Leadership Characteristics 81
Balance (Life)—All Things in Proportion 85

ABOUT THE AUTHOR

Mike Holt is a businessman, educator, author, speaker, software designer and Code expert. His interest in business began in the early 70's when he opened a successful contracting firm. With the skills he gained contracting, he launched his second business, Concepts in Electricity, a school dedicated to teaching electrical contractors. Mike went on to start a software company that specialized in estimating software and eventually brought all of his businesses under the umbrella of Mike Holt Enterprises. This experience in several different types of companies has given him a broad perspective on building a profitable business that is committed to its customers and to quality.

From an early age Mike understood the need for working on your business, not just in your business, in addition to the need for continuous education in order to stay current and competitive. It is that knowledge, coupled with his experience in the field and the running of a profitable business for over 40 years that gives him a unique perspective that provides the foundation for this textbook.

Mike attended the University of Miami's Graduate School for a Master's in Business Administration. This program gave him the knowledge to take his business to the next level. The skills that he developed throughout all of this experience helped him build one of the most successful business management workshops in the electrical industry. He has helped thousands of electrical contractors improve their businesses by becoming more effective, focusing on the essentials, improving their management skills and learning effective strategies to grow themselves personally in addition to growing their business.

Companies across the United States have utilized Mike's services for in-house training and expert advice. His unsurpassed speaking ability has been a source of encouragement to companies and agencies such as ATT, IBM, Boeing, NECA, IAEI, IBEW, ICBO, the U.S. Navy, Grand Coulee Dam, and even the government of Mexico. Mike's appeal lies in his ability to teach a variety of subjects to individuals that have different degrees of expertise. This workbook is an example of how he can help individuals learn regardless of their current knowledge level. He motivates people to be the best they can be, and take their skills to the next level.

Mike resides in Central Florida, is the father of seven children, and has many outside interests and activities. He is an eight-time National Barefoot Water-Ski Champion (1988, 1999, 2005, 2006, 2007, 2008, 2009, and 2012) and has set many national records. In 2015, at the age of 63, Mike started a new career in competitive mountain bike racing. Lots of bumps and bruises but he's having a wonderful time. He continues to find ways to motivate himself mentally and physically. What sets Mike apart from many is his commitment to living a balanced lifestyle; he places God first, then family, career, and self.

PREFACE

When I first started, I don't remember having dreams or goals, and certainly I never imagined I would end up here—with who I am and what I have created. What I do know, is that no matter what my job was, I was always committed to doing the best that I could. I was hungry, and I always put myself in a position to learn everything that I could, so that I could do my job independently and then take it to the next level. Sure I made mistakes, but that's how I learned. When I was a job foreman I made sure that I knew the scope of the job; I made sure I knew everyone's needs. I took care of the builder, the inspector, the supply house and the trades. And guess what? My boss never came to the jobsite. Why? Because he knew that I took total responsibility, and that I had it covered. I made sure that I did the work so that everyone else's job was easier. I gave them all the tools.

You are 100 percent responsible for the job that you do. Your goal should be to have total complete control in the scope of work, whatever your job. At times you may be in over your head. If you don't know, ask. Find a mentor. Listen to conversations around you. Seek job training. Ask yourself what you need to do to take over full responsibility of your job, and do whatever it takes to get there.

Whatever your dream is, you need basic skills to be employable and somewhat successful. Maybe you never had the opportunity to be taught, or weren't encouraged to make something of yourself. But you need to cover the fundamentals. Maybe you're not looking to be in charge. Maybe you just lack the confidence to think about yourself as a leader. Start by doing some of the things that leaders do, and help and encourage the people around you. Others will react to your behavior and they'll start to respond to you differently. You'll feel the validation.

It might be a leap of faith—but you have to take risks. You'll find that the small wins add up, success begets success, and build on that momentum. But don't get cocky, there's a danger in that. Just remember to be humble and focused on the core values.

To lead is to serve. If you make it your goal to do the best that you can and to help people, then you can't fail. Put yourself in a position where you do everything you can to know your job well, commit to keep learning, and you're guaranteed success. You're already on the right track—if for no other reason, you're reading this book!

Notes

INTRODUCTION

Being a leader is about living your life in a way that inspires or encourages others. Leadership has to do with the day-to-day choices you make to succeed in your personal life or in your work. It's about being the best you can be, no matter what part of your career you're in or what stage of life. Regardless of whether you currently lead others or even plan to someday, you can make choices that will have great impact on all areas of your life and help you be an example to those around you.

If you ask people who they think of when they think of a leader, they might reel off a list of names of charismatic, well-known people they see on the news, but the signs of outstanding leadership appear all around you every day. Leaders are the ones who are:

- Reaching their full potential
- Continuously learning
- Serving others
- Achieving results
- Managing conflict appropriately
- Changing with grace

Are you born with leadership skills or can they be learned? **Rest assured—the skills that make true leaders can be developed just like any skill.** Some people will find that leadership skills come easily, while others will find they have to work hard at them and continuously practice, but everyone has the capability. We regard leadership as a quality that bestows power, commands respect, and fosters achievement. We sometimes come across people who exhibit these qualities early in life, and we might say "they're a born leader," but generally these skills are carefully cultivated over the course of a lifetime, rather than the result of a genetic lottery.

The ultimate compliment in today's society is to be considered a leader, but the demands of being one are significant and impact not only yourself, but others around you. Leadership entails sacrifice, dedication, focus, hard work and long hours, and can be a lonely journey. It puts you in a position of being in the spotlight, of becoming a "visible target." People might turn against you if your decisions aren't to their liking, so to be effective you'll want to develop a thick skin.

A leader's role is to provide and maintain momentum and clarity, whether the focal point is an organization, sports team, group of volunteers, family, or personal life. This momentum will come if you have a clear vision of the end goal. You'll need a well thought-out strategy to achieve that vision, along with a carefully formulated and communicated plan. The plan must foster and enable everyone involved, and you'll need to be accountable for achieving those goals. To maintain this momentum, and grow, you'll find there's give and take, and you'll find there are times when you need to be willing to allow others to lead you.

Introduction

A significant factor in your success is having a support group. Ideally, you'll want to find your encouragement and positive reinforcement from family, close friends, and business associates, but this is not always possible. If you can't find support from those around you, you'll need to go elsewhere. Seek out like-minded individuals so you can discuss ideas and share opinions and goals that will help you succeed.

The rewards of leadership are many, and this textbook will provide a great opportunity for you to develop your own vision of the type of leader you want to become.

If you are currently leading others, use this textbook for inspiration and ideas to train your team to become the next generation of leaders.

Our goal is to assist you in recognizing, developing, and improving on the skills that will help you become a successful player in your own life—being in control of your own destiny, whatever you determine that to be. To achieve even a modest level of success requires total participation and commitment on your part—no-one else can do this work for you. Set an example others can follow with pride.

SECTION 1
PERSONAL BRANDING

Introduction

Normally when we think about branding, we think about symbols or signs that define companies or products. When we think of a brand we might think of McDonald's, Apple, or Coca-Cola. A brand isn't a concept that we're used to thinking about on a personal level. Personal branding has been described as "self-packaging," a way of presenting and positioning yourself in your life and your career. It's part of developing yourself as a leader, and those people who take it seriously help themselves stand out in a positive way.

Who are you?
How do you want to be perceived by others?
How do you make yourself memorable?

This is your personal brand, and is your promise to your family, your friends, your employer, your coworkers, and your subordinates. It differentiates you from others and lets people know what they can expect from you. It should reflect your true best self and how you would like others to see you. Your personal "brand" should answer questions like:

- What do you stand for?
- What are your values?
- What's your vision for yourself?

Your personal brand includes everything from your appearance, to your smile, your handshake, and how you conduct yourself. We quite often send the wrong message because we don't think about these things or how they might impact the way others see us. This section explores all of the ways you can make an impact by cultivating your personal brand.

The Personal Branding Traits Included in This Section are:

Appearance	4
Attitude	6
Conduct	8
Confidence	9
Reputation	11

Section 1 | Personal Branding

APPEARANCE

First impressions are lasting ones, and you want your first one to send the message that you're a leader. Your appearance should convey an impression of success. Research has shown that when a person likes one aspect of a thing (whether it's something about you, an organization, company, or anything else) they'll tend to think positively about all aspects of that thing. It's called the "Halo Effect." Conversely, if they dislike an aspect of something, they'll tend to think negatively about the whole thing. Utilize the "halo effect" to your advantage by making a great first impression and setting yourself up for success.

The way you groom and present yourself to the world sends a message. Some people focus on that message only when they're looking for a job, but true leaders think about their professional appearance at all times—even after they have the job and when they're the ones doing the hiring. Your appearance is always important.

Clothing. Choose your clothing based on your position and where you are in your career. Obviously, someone working a trade in the field will dress differently than someone who works in an office, as an outside salesperson, or as the owner of a business. Make sure your clothes are always clean, pressed and in good repair, even if you're wearing a uniform. Things like this matter. Make sure you dress for respect. Sometimes what's appropriate for the job may cost more than your budget allows. If this is the case look for sales or go to thrift shops. Don't let your budget stop you from dressing suitably for your job.

> The way you groom and present yourself to the world sends a message.

You should always dress at the top of the range for your position. If you work a trade in the field, wear jeans and polo shirts instead of shorts and t-shirts or jeans with holes in them; jeans should NEVER fall below your hips and shirts should always be tasteful. If you work in an office environment, it will be wise to select dressier clothing—you'll take your cue based on the dress code of the company. If you're the owner, make sure you determine what image you want to project. Establish a dress code for the company and then be sure you dress in the way that represents that image and sets the example. This applies equally to men and women.

Body Art. Although tattoos and body piercings have become quite common, you should consider your long-term goals if you're thinking about getting body art. Tattoos are permanent and their location and style can affect how you're seen on the job or as a leader. If your goal is to be the CEO of a large contracting firm someday, remember that some people may be conservative and visible tattoos might create a negative impression. If you already have one or more, you should do your best to cover them up and you'll find it easier to avoid or overcome negative stereotyping. In short, it's wise for you to consider your career and leadership goals before choosing to invest in tattoos or body piercings.

> People who take the time to look professional make a better impression.

Hygiene. As important as clothing is to the impression you make, so is your personal hygiene. It seems obvious, but it's worth mentioning how important cleanliness is. People notice the condition of your teeth whenever you smile, they notice if you appear not to have bathed, and for sure they notice if your use of cologne, perfume, or aftershave is excessive. There are many people who are allergic to strong scents and will be uncomfortable in your presence—"less is more." Pay attention to the length of your hair and your general grooming. People who take the time to look professional usually make a better impression than those who don't.

Section 1 | Personal Branding

ATTITUDE

Everyone notices a powerful and positive attitude. What you think and believe about yourself shows in the way you walk, stand, and communicate with people. Do everything you can to develop and maintain a positive attitude about your ability to be successful and your ability to accomplish your objectives. People respond well to a positive attitude.

Success itself doesn't come overnight—it's a process through which each of us must go. But believing in your success and acting the part can start on day one. By taking the time to study or learn something new every day, success can be achieved. Your public school years were a process. You didn't go from Kindergarten to Graduation Day in 30 minutes, a week, or even a year. If you understand that success won't come "overnight" (because you understand it's a process) then you won't be disappointed, frustrated, or disillusioned.

Sure, you'll encounter problems, but everyone does. What distinguishes a leader is how they react. There are problems and challenges to every endeavor, and everyone has to overcome difficulties. Make it a practice to keep your attention on your work and be positive about your job, and you'll be able to cope with and overcome any problems that arise. Welcome adversity as a learning experience.

> **People respond well to a positive attitude.**

We all have "bad" days and "good" days—it happens. But one of the most important things you must learn to do is to develop a positive attitude, especially at those times when it seems the most difficult. Be cheerful and upbeat even on days when you don't really feel that way. You're 100 percent in charge of choosing your attitude, and you can choose a positive one. Ability, capability, and availability of resources will go far toward making success possible but without a positive attitude they're wasted, and success, if any, will be incomplete and unfulfilling.

Don't spend your time and effort worrying—that feeds negative energy into your life. Worrying feeds the belief that you'll fail, or that the worst thing will happen to you. Faith and a positive attitude are essential to succeeding. Make a commitment to think positively and give your best effort at all times. Focus on what you have, not on what you lack, and maximize your best assets. Be thankful to God for your opportunities and abilities. Live a life of thankfulness instead of worry.

Surround yourself with friends and family members who support your goals and your mission. Unfortunately, sometimes people in our group have negative attitudes; don't allow them to influence you or to advise you in any way.

Key elements in developing a great (winning) attitude are **belief, desire, and expectancy**.

- A winner **believes** they can win no matter what. They believe they're worthy and deserve to win. There's an old saying that's applicable here—"As you believe, so shall you be."

- Winners always have a burning **desire** to win. Their desire to win is what makes them winners. To quote another cliché—"A winner never quits and quitters never win."

- Finally, winners **expect** to win no matter what the conditions are. Fear, while natural, is negative expectancy—expecting not to win. Confidence is positive expectancy—knowing you're going to win.

> How you approach each day is your choice.

These three elements can't be tested or measured. They're all subjective and internal, but they can all work together to help you develop a winning, positive attitude. How you approach each day is your choice.

CONDUCT

Your conduct is one of the first things about you that people notice.

If you want others to see you in a positive light, surround yourself with people who are already viewed that way. Think about those people you choose to hang around with. Are they well spoken? Do they constantly use profanity when they speak? Are they responsible or unreliable? Does their conduct command respect? If the goal of your friends isn't the same as yours, you'll need to distance yourself from them a bit, and make sure you associate with people who have the same aspirations as you do. As you grow you might lose old friends, but you'll make new ones. Stick to your commitments to yourself and to serve others, and you'll be surprised to discover how many of your friends grow with you! Let your conduct instill confidence of others in you.

> Our conduct says a lot more to the world about us than our words.

Just as you can choose to have a positive attitude, you can choose to conduct yourself as a respected, reliable, knowledgeable person with integrity. This is important if you want to succeed. You might not have the right role models around you to learn from, but start to observe successful people, especially leaders in your industry. Notice the way they enter a room, what impresses you about them, and how they interact with other individuals with assurance and confidence. Their successful habits can become yours.

In life we can't always control the events around us, but we can always control the way we react to them. Our conduct says a lot more to the world about us than our words. You should ask yourself what your conduct is saying about you every day.

CONFIDENCE

Being confident in yourself and your abilities is vital. You need to realize that you not only can, but also will have success when you work hard and work smart. Three things that are significant in gaining the level of self-confidence you need are **competence, commitment, and control.**

- **Competence** is built by doing your homework. You can't slow down and expect to succeed if you haven't studied for a test you must take. The only way to have confidence is to know you've done your best to be prepared. Build competence by starting from an expectation of success. Mentally rehearse success. See, feel, and hear the desired end result. Put positive pressure on yourself to create the outcome you desire. When you do the work and build your competence it gives you confidence and is immediately recognized by others.

> See, feel, and hear the desired end result.

- **Commitment** to the task. Decide what it is you want and then be committed to its completion. All projects have obstacles that stand in the way; commit to working long enough and hard enough that you're able to see your project through to the end. Putting a little bit more work into achieving these goals builds your confidence in yourself and your ability to succeed on larger projects in the future. **Work smart not just hard.** This simple premise is no guarantee for success, but it's the only way performance will be maximized. With smart, hard work, there's always a chance to succeed. Without it, failure is guaranteed.

- **Control** your responses. As you handle challenges or begin a project, you might notice reactions in your body—an increase in heart rate, a dry mouth, a hollow feeling in the pit of your stomach, or muscle tightness. These are normal feelings providing notice that your body and mind are ready to meet the challenge. They aren't an indication of impending failure—nothing can be accomplished without some amount of tension. Work on taking control of your responses including your emotions and thoughts. There will be factors you won't be able to control so don't waste time worrying about them. Just concentrate on the ones over which you can exercise some degree of influence. Use this natural tension to help you steer the ship instead of worrying about failure.

There's a theory called "self-fulfilling prophecy" that can help you build a strong positive self-image. When you anticipate performance of a certain caliber, it's likely you'll perform according to those expectations regardless of your skills. If you have minimal skills and a less than confident self-perception, look for ways to improve.

Section 1 | Personal Branding

> Walk the walk and talk the talk—and, your confidence will continue to increase.

Remember that your confidence will be built by your competence; developing your self-confidence through education, experience, and even failures will help you overcome any inhibitions or shyness you might feel. As your skill level grows, chances are your performance will improve at the same time. People like to do business with, and depend on confident people so develop and manage an image that creates an air of confidence. Walk the walk and talk the talk—and, your confidence will continue to increase.

REPUTATION

Your reputation is produced by the impressions you make on others with your actions and how they're perceived over time.

Live a life that builds a positive reputation in all of your endeavors, both personally and professionally. Endangering others by doing shoddy work, cutting corners, not following through on promises, or having a poor attitude, causes you to lose the confidence and respect of those around you and rebuilding your reputation and relationships is very difficult, if not impossible.

Your reputation is critical to your success. An image can be "cleaned up" over time, but your reputation—not so easy. Your reputation must always be guarded and protected. Cultivate honesty, fairness, and quality work in everything that you do—with your employer, employees, customers, and peers. Establishing a good reputation is the key to progressing to the next level. Word-of-mouth is one of the most powerful sources behind getting a job whether it's employment or a contract for services. You can't expect a good reference from an unsatisfied employer or customer.

> An image can be "cleaned up" over time, but your reputation—not so easy.

Of course, we all make mistakes. It's important to recognize when one has been made. When they happen, face the consequences, and commit yourself to learning from them. For example, you might not follow through on a promise you made, or you might have had a bad day that resulted in a bad attitude. The first thing to do is apologize. Next, figure out the reason it happened and take steps to prevent the same thing from happening again. The key is to minimize actions that damage your image and reputation.

How good is your reputation? Generally, how do you think those around you would describe your reputation? What would you expect it to be—good, fair, or bad? What might have caused you to have a less than desirable reputation? Take some time and ask for honest opinions. Whatever you do, don't be angry if it's not as good as you think it should be. Be humble, and take steps to improve. On the other hand, you might be pleasantly surprised by good things that might be said.

Your *integrity* is the foundation of your reputation. This doesn't mean you need to be squeaky clean and have no enemies. What it does mean is that you need to strive, from this point forward, to be principled, and keep your integrity as strong as possible.

Conclusion

Improving and building up your own self-image, self-worth, character, and reputation dramatically affects how you're perceived.

Your personal brand is a work in progress. Initially it might be defined by the clothes you can afford to wear, or the way in which you cut or wear your hair. This is a part of it, but not the whole story. Your vision for yourself might constantly change as you learn and recognize what drives you, but you should be committed to doing your best.

Your goal for your personal brand should be whatever it takes to build the respect and the reputation to help you accomplish your goals.

SECTION 2
DEVELOPING BASIC SKILLS

Introduction

If one of your goals is to be a leader or part of a company's management team, or have a business of your own, you'll need to sharpen your current skills and learn new ones. If your goal isn't to lead, but to have a great career, then managing your time and managing your skills will still do much to create a great opportunity for contributing to your long-term success.

You should undertake long-range planning to achieve your goals and growth expectations, and short-range planning to stay busy, pay the bills, and build up financial reserves. It's just as important to apply these skills to your personal life to help you succeed in achieving your personal goals.

There are some basic rules that, when practiced, will make your work easier:

- Know your objectives (what you want to achieve).
- Plan your strategies (how you're going to achieve it).

The Basic Skills Covered in This Section are:

Communication	14
Goal Setting	17
"NO"—the Most Difficult Word	21
Organization	22
Planning	23
Relating to Your Customers	25
Teamwork	27
Time Management	28

COMMUNICATION

To be able to communicate properly is an important basic life skill and is especially essential for anyone that's a leader, or aspiring to become one. As a leader, you must be able to congratulate, console, confront, motivate, and teach your team in a variety of ways. You have to keep them engaged and productive, inspire them to achieve their full potential, and solidify your relationship with the entire group. It's essential to develop good communication skills for that to happen.

Think about how often you talk to someone and think they don't understand you; or vice versa. When you're communicating with someone, you need to know what that person means, not just what they say. Think about it. The meaning behind the words is just as important as what's being said. It's important in reverse too. You need to make sure when you're speaking to a person that they understand what you really mean.

> Be sure the message is clear—once sent it's hard to retract.

Communication is a two-way street. When you're having a conversation with another person are you listening or are you just waiting for your turn to speak? Too many times people are thinking about their own response while the other person is still talking and they don't listen carefully enough. When you're listening, stay focused on what the other person is saying, repeat some of what they say to show that you're really paying attention. Ask questions to clarify something if you don't understand what they mean. If they're asking you a question, concentrate, and ask yourself what it is they're really asking for. Listen closely when they're speaking. Don't try to formulate your answer while the question is still being asked. Wait and pay attention. This will not only improve your understanding but will also make you a superior listener and earn people's respect. The value of listening can't be underestimated. Good listening is a skill that requires practice and it often doesn't come naturally. Leaders who listen well set a positive example for their followers and provide a foundation for a strong relationship. "A mind is like a parachute—it works best when it's open!"

Face-to-Face Communication. Some conversations are better face to face. This lets you see each other's reactions, facial expressions, body language and gestures. It gives you immediate feedback, so you know how to proceed with your conversation. It builds a connection that may be difficult to achieve with a text message or email. When you're the one doing the talking, watch the other person's expression and body language. Doing so will give you a sense of what they're feeling, and you'll know if they understand what you're saying. If you see that they're not following you, don't get frustrated. Find another way to say what you mean. Maybe you're talking too fast, so pause occasionally when sharing your ideas to make sure you're communicating at a pace that's comfortable for your listener. This is especially important when sharing new ideas. Notice individual differences.

Take the time to observe people with whom you associate regularly. This will help you become familiar with their communication style, individual mannerisms, and their body language. Being aware and respectful of cultural differences is especially important here.

Telephone Communication. When talking on the telephone (especially a cell phone), be sure to speak clearly. Use the speaker only when absolutely necessary. Since you can't see each other, true communication might be a little more difficult because neither of you can "read" the other's expression or body language. Be careful about making a negative assumption about the other's tone of voice—it can be easy to misunderstand what the "tone" you hear means. If you think they might not have understood what you said, ask them. If you aren't sure of what they're saying, let them know. You can also say something like, "I think you're telling me. . ." and then repeat back what you believe you're being told.

Written Communication. Writing includes letters, notes, emails, and text messages. Before sending something off in writing, take the time to read it over. Be sure the message is clear—once sent it's hard to retract! Remember that you know what your intention is when you are writing, but unless you express that clearly, the reader will have no idea! Be sure your spelling and grammar are as correct as possible. Check to make sure that there aren't important words missing. Remember that you're projecting an image through this type of communication.

> **Being organized not only save you time but reduces your stress.**

- Use the correct combination of upper- and lower-case letters in anything you write—even if it's an email or text message. Avoid abbreviations and slang as the recipient might not know what they mean. Knowing how to type is a big plus because it allows you to produce written communications more quickly, but if you're using a mobile device, read it before you send it because the auto-correct feature might have changed words you were not trying to write.
- How's your handwriting? Can people read it? Are others coming to you to find out what you wrote? Are they spending time trying to decipher what you've written, or taking a wild guess about it? If others can't read what you've written, you aren't communicating effectively. Valuable time will be wasted, and mistakes will occur. If legible handwriting isn't one of your current skills, begin practicing your penmanship to improve it.

If you're sharing bad or unpleasant news, think very carefully about which form of communication you choose—you might not want to send negative content via a written communication. You want to be sure people understand the true meaning of the information you're relaying. Talking to them in person might be the most appropriate way because you can control your attitude, expression, and tone of voice. On the other hand, there are times where it's necessary to have a written record no matter the topic. When this is the case, be cautious with your choice of words and style of writing.

Section 2 | Developing Basic Skills

Thinking Out Loud. If you're in the habit of thinking out loud, people around you might be confused—they won't know whether you're suggesting something, expressing a random thought, or making a decision. As a result, they may take action on something you said without realizing that wasn't your intention, and you were only mulling over ideas out loud. If you find that you do think out loud, be careful to let people around you know what you are doing so that they know whether or not they should disregard the statements you make. Remember—he who's in control of his tongue possesses great wisdom!

Never use profanity—there's absolutely no place for it. It's very offensive to many people, and its regular use can be perceived as a lack of education or a lack of self-control. If you routinely use profanity in your conversations with friends or family, make it a point to change that habit! Record conversations and then play them back to hear how often you use curse words. You can also ask someone to say something whenever you use them—doing so will help you become more aware and allow you to develop the habit of using different words.

> He who's in control of his tongue possesses great wisdom!

Reading skills are a basic part of the communication process and are very important. How well can you read? Is it easy for you to understand what you've read? If your reading skills are weak, you might be making mistakes because of your lack of understanding written information. Make the commitment to improve. Read books in your leisure time, enrich your vocabulary by looking up words and phrases that are new to you, and get help if necessary.

There's a basic truth to achieving success as a leader. You must know how to handle people, how to handle problems, and you must know how to handle yourself. Don't underestimate the importance of communication.

GOAL SETTING

Everyone at some time talks about things they'd like to achieve in their career or in their personal life. Some are quite ambitious—"I'd like to start my own business and be listed in the Fortune 500." Some are seemingly minor—"I'd like to clean out my tool box so when I go looking for something, I can find it easily."

There are different types of goals: **health-related goals** (quit smoking, exercise daily, lose weight); **personal goals** (be a water-ski champion, increase my bowling average, buy a house, get a new car); **spiritual goals** (establish a better relationship with my family, attend religious services on a regular basis); and **career goals** (get a promotion, a raise, additional training).

You set goals because there's an aspect of your life or work that you want to improve. Setting goals and following through can be difficult, not only because doing so forces you to objectively evaluate each goal you choose to set, but also because it requires a commitment (sometimes an extraordinary commitment) to follow through and achieve that goal.

To achieve success, you must be sure your goals are driven by your own personal values, and then you can concentrate on becoming result oriented. Have a sense of the mission you're trying to complete. Assess your own strengths and limitations objectively. Think hard about your goals, and consider any financial resources that might be needed, as well as compromises and sacrifices that may have to be made. Determine if this is something you really want to accomplish—then **DO** it!

> Be sure your goals are driven by your own personal values.

Goal Setting 101—the SMART method. When selecting goals many people recommend using the SMART method. It's a method that gives you a better chance of success and has repeatedly proven to be effective. Here's what a SMART goal looks like:

- **S** = **Specific**. Your goal should be specific and not general. An example is "I want to lose 20 lbs." versus "I want to lose weight."

- **M** = **Measurable**. Your goal should be able to be measured by others. An example is "I want to lower my blood pressure to xyz." versus "I want better health."

- **A** = **Achievable**. Are there steps you can take to make it happen? Is it actionable?

- **R** = **Realistic**. If you're middle aged and haven't picked up a basketball in 10 years, then making a goal to be a professional basketball player probably isn't something that can be achieved. Your goals should be lofty but based on reality.

- **T** = **Time Based**. When do you want the complete your goal? A good goal has a deadline.

Using the SMART method will help you set goals that are easier to achieve than if you simply write down generalized ideas.

Section 2 | Developing Basic Skills

The First Step is to Identify Your Goals—Right Now! Procrastination is one of the biggest barriers to effective goal setting. Yes, it's usually easier to "do it later" or to "do it tomorrow." Remember "later" and "tomorrow" are always later; so do it now!! Make a strong effort and commitment to make every moment count. Ask yourself questions like:

- What does success mean to me?
- What are the five most important things in my life?
- What do I want to accomplish in my work?
- What do I want to accomplish in my home?
- What do I want to accomplish for myself?

There are three different types of goals; **short-range goals**, **intermediate goals**, and **long-range/lifetime goals**. Make a list of everything you've ever considered doing or accomplishing. Your list can include topics ranging from business, financial, family, spiritual, physical, or mental goals. Use a "brainstorming" form to write down everything you've ever considered being, doing, or having. Include as many things on your list as you wish. Even "off the wall" goals belong here, because they have value too and can be used as a starting point for establishing others. To really get your goal-setting process started, try to list 50 goals you want to accomplish in your life. This process will help you get out of the box and help you identify what you really want to achieve and what success looks like for you.

> Write down everything you've ever considered being, doing, or having.

The next step is to identify which goals you want to accomplish first because you can't reach all of them at the same time. Examine each goal to decide whether it's short-range (can be accomplished in one year or less), intermediate (can be accomplished in one to five years), or a long-range or lifetime goal. Set a realistic date of achievement for each of them and write them down. Once the list is made, don't put it in a drawer and forget about it. Place it in your bedroom, perhaps on a mirror, so you'll look at it every day. To achieve goals, you must be willing to make the commitment to follow through. Review your goal sheets at least once a month. **Work hard! Do it now!**

Next, realistically evaluate the present status for each of the goals you've selected and create a list of steps and strategies that will help you reach them on paper or on your computer. Writing them out will help you think through your goals and give you a great place to reference as you work toward them.

For instance, if one of your goals is to develop a strong understanding of the National Electrical Code®, seek the advice of your employer or supervisor about effective learning tools and tips. Develop a list of the steps you're going to take to achieve this goal. Your list might look like this:

1. Purchase a Code book and tabs.
2. Tab my Code book.
3. Keep my Code book in my car so that I can reference it while out in the field and highlight important articles.
4. Join a Code forum so that I can post questions about parts of the Code book I don't understand.
5. Purchase a Code training program so that I can learn all of the parts of my Code book with formalized training.
6. Set aside time each week to work on my knowledge of the Code.
7. Find a mentor in the field who's a Code expert and bounce ideas off them when I get to a gray area.
8. Take a Code update class.

If your goal is to learn a new sport, enlist the help of a coach or personal trainer who can lay the groundwork properly. If you've set a goal to become more tolerant with family and friends, ask them how they perceive you and what they believe you think of, and feel about them. This is no time to "flinch" from criticism. Understand that you're asking a question and you must be willing to receive the answers without responding negatively to the feedback—whatever it might be. This step in creating your game plan is the most important action you can take to see where you are and where you need to go. From these exchanges and strategy brainstorming sessions, you can better determine where you are and be better able to determine approximately how long it will take you to achieve your goal. Decide if you'll need additional formal training, professional counseling, or coaching-type help. Research the methods needed to achieve your goals, and plan your completion date accordingly.

> As a confidence builder, start by selecting short-range goals.

Select at Least Two Goals That You'll Work on Every Day. It will be easier to select them if you remember that you must answer "yes" to these five questions about each.

1. Is it really my personal goal?
2. Is it morally right and fair to everyone?
3. If the goal is a short-range step, is it consistent with my long-range or lifetime goals?
4. Can I emotionally commit myself to start and finish the project?
5. Can I see myself achieving this objective?

As a confidence builder, especially if you've never set goals before, start by selecting short-range goals you know you can reach in one month or so.

Section 2 | Developing Basic Skills

To share or not to share! Another decision you'll have to make when setting your goals is whether or not you should share them with others. If they're "**give up**" goals; that is, give up smoking, cursing, drinking too much, and so on, almost everyone will provide you with encouragement to help you stay on track. Share your goals carefully if they're "**go up**" goals; such as, earning a promotion, successfully negotiating an increase in compensation, starting your own business, making the team number one, and so forth. For lifetime goals, make certain you're committed to them before you share your ideas with anyone. Talk with those who are important to you and are generally positive and supportive people, and ask for their support in achieving these types of goals. Once you've achieved some success, you can share them with family members, friends, or co-workers.

> To achieve even a minor level of success, decide what must be done and then do it.

As a Leader, You Might Set Goals For Others. This requires a fine balance between creating a goal that will give incentives for them to extend themselves beyond their current abilities, but not so remote that reaching it will be beyond their ability to achieve and create a feeling of frustration and apathy. Ambitious people typically react favorably to a challenge. As a leader, your job is to set attainable goals, provide direction, support, and encouragement. You must make people believe you have confidence in their abilities and have faith that they'll achieve the desired end result. When you include them in the goal setting process, you obtain a buy-in, a greater commitment to the goal, and a consensus of the responsibility for achievement.

To achieve even a minor level of success, decide what must be done and then do it. Ideas are important and they're necessary, but they're only the beginning. Ideas must be carried out to have meaning. Something that remains in your mind doesn't do anyone any good. If you fail to plan, you plan to fail. This is one of the reasons it's so important for leaders to manage their own time. You must attend to your day-to-day functions, and you must also set aside time to think and make plans. That's your job as a leader, and if you don't do it—no one else will!

Setting goals for personal improvement means that you're willing to do whatever's necessary to move forward. Don't let your life be filled with regrets and "if onlys." Make up your mind to do the things that you truly feel will better your life. If you really want to improve your quality of life, whatever the goal, make the commitment and—**GO** for it! "No pain, no gain!" so the saying goes, but so too does it follow that no potential loss, no potential benefit.

"NO"—THE MOST DIFFICULT WORD

They say it's our ability to say "No" that determines how successful we truly are in life. Have you ever found yourself saying "yes" when you really wanted to say "no"? It's something almost everyone does and we do it for a variety of reasons. We don't want to hurt someone's feelings. We don't want to appear uncooperative. We're afraid people won't like us if we say "no."

Remember that part of being a leader is being honest, so don't say "yes" or "maybe" when you want to say "no." Be assertive, not deceptive. Don't agree with something you can't do or don't want to do. Don't take on a responsibility for which you have no obligation. Don't let yourself be talked into doing anything that's contrary to your best interests or those of the team. You'll reduce your stress level by saying "no" to a situation you can't handle, or don't choose to handle. Say "no" and mean it!

Consider what you're actually able to do versus what you would like to do. There's nothing wrong with saying "no" if you know that added responsibility will cause a serious problem with your schedule. A survey suggested that if you were to say "no," it would be the correct answer 80 percent of the time. When you do say "yes" and make a commitment, be realistic about the expectations and the time needed to complete or honor it.

> Our ability to say "no" determines how successful we truly are in life.

Even though it might be difficult at first, with practice you'll find it easier to draw the line tactfully and protect your time. Said correctly, people usually respond well to a firm "no." It requires clear, logical thinking. Don't be wishy-washy! Be honest about whatever you decide to do. Explain why you can't (or won't) agree to the request. If there are alternatives, share them with the other person. Most people will appreciate your honesty.

Section 2 | Developing Basic Skills

ORGANIZATION

Keeping your schedule and your workspace orderly and systematic is the only way you're going to be as productive and effective as you can be. Being disorganized results in a perpetual cycle that becomes so overwhelming that you don't know where to even begin to clean it up. More often than not, you just won't do it; you'll walk away and do something else. Don't put it off. Break it down into smaller manageable pieces and do it in stages.

Looking for misplaced items wastes time and reduces your productivity. If your office is stacked so high with piles of stuff that you can't see your desk, or there's such a mess in your truck that you can't see the floor, then you won't be able to find anything when you need it. You definitely won't be able to get the job done efficiently.

> Being organized not only save you time but reduces your stress.

Find a place for everything, whether it be physical items, books and papers or electronic information. Invest in filing cabinets, storage boxes or bookcases and label them. If you don't have the time or the discipline, or even the skills, find an assistant or a colleague to partner with you. Organize it, put it away, or get rid of it, if it's not necessary to keep. You'll be able to focus on the job at hand if that's all you have in your line of sight.

Having everything organized and at your fingertips will save you time when working on any project and allow you to use that time for other projects or for a much-needed break. Not only can being organized reduce your stress, but it might also allow you to work more energetically.

Identify any areas where you feel you need help in getting organized, whether it's with your workspace, your filing system or your appointment calendar. Get books or look for articles on the internet that address those specific needs; you'll find tips, ideas and guides that can "change your life." If you feel especially overwhelmed, hire an organizational expert in your area to help you create systems to keep your work space organized. Decluttering can be cathartic and free you up to do things you would never have thought you had time for.

Organizing the things around you will reduce your stress and improve the amount of control you feel you have in your work and life. You certainly won't be a leading example for anyone on your team if you or your workspace looks disorganized. So, make a commitment today to be the type of leader who has created an organized environment and great organizational systems.

PLANNING

The key to being ready to work, and to being able to have a productive day, week, or year is to plan. You need to work with an uncluttered mind like you do with an uncluttered workspace.

There are a few basic rules to follow when planning:

1. Write things down and have a master to-do list in one place.

2. Review all of your notes and to-dos on a regular basis and constantly update the list with each task.

3. Know your priorities based on your goals.

4. Schedule time to organize your weeks, months, and year; what items on your to-do lists have a time deadline? Which items have to happen first? What are you trying to accomplish?

Face it. If you don't write things down, there'll be something you'll forget. Have you ever gone to the grocery store to pick up some soda, then discover after you leave that you bought some other things and forgot the soda? The same thing happens with tasks that need to be accomplished. Our schedules are just so busy, and there are so many things to be done, that we can't remember everything. How many times have you found yourself in a sticky situation because you forgot to do something? If you're like most people, it's probably been quite often.

> **If you don't write things down, there'll be something you'll forget.**

Once you've made your plans and lists, cross out those things that are done. Anything not finished should be carried over to the next day and placed at the top of the list if possible. Eliminate anything that's no longer needed. Look at every action you take and determine if it's helping you reach your goals. If it isn't, don't do it!

- Set objectives and deadlines.

- Delegate responsibility and accountability.

- Utilize commercially available organizers, such as smart phones or tablets to help make better use of your time.

If there are any schedule conflicts, resolve them as early as possible. If you have something to do and can't get it done, plan to complete it the next day or at the next available opportunity. Never allow one missed appointment to cause a delay for the remainder of the day. Apologize, reschedule, and continue through the day.

> Organize your time and plan wisely.

Studies have shown that using a paper-and-pen planning method actually improves outcomes. The feel of the paper, and the act of writing your priorities on lists helps you organize your mind as you're doing it, and makes you think of additional things relevant to the project as you're writing. For some people, there's something positive about carrying a small notebook or an index card with their plans for the day in their own handwriting. Once you've mapped out what you want to accomplish you need to get it on your calendar and commit to it daily.

Organize your time and plan wisely. One of our greatest faults is not being disciplined with our schedules. Staying busy and working very long hours doesn't equal effective productivity or leadership.

RELATING TO YOUR CUSTOMERS

Without customers, we wouldn't have a job or an income. Whether you're on a job as the owner or as an employee representing the company, to the customer you're the face of the company. The customer will notice all of the things we've already talked about; your appearance, your attitude, and the way you speak to others. They'll form an opinion of the business you represent based on all of these factors. Be the person to set the example of how to treat customers properly. This one skill will set you apart as a leader in the field.

Always treat customers with respect—no matter what! Always be pleasant. Maintain a professional image even under adverse conditions. Sometimes things can become a bit unpleasant. If a conflict develops between you and a customer, stay calm and don't lose your temper. Make sure that you allow the customer to finish what they have to say without interrupting them—let them express their full complaint or concerns before you start to offer a solution. This allows them to feel that they are being heard. If the issue is something you can't resolve, and you're an employee then direct the customer to your supervisor rather than trying to "fix" the situation yourself. If you can, observe the manner in which your supervisor responds so you can learn from the experience.

NEVER allow yourself to be unpleasant or disrespectful to a customer. If a conflict develops between a customer and someone else, stay out of it! Never take it personally even when a customer is wrong about what they're saying; simply listen and calmly state your position in a respectful way.

If customers are unfair and attack you or the company, if you're angry or your feelings are hurt, you might have a tendency to shout back or say something inappropriate or disrespectful. If you feel like this, count to ten before you say anything; better yet (especially if you're REALLY hurt or angry), wait at least 24 hours before you say anything. That will give you a chance to calm down and think about the best way to handle the situation.

> **Make sure you allow the customer to feel that they are being heard.**

Always remember that words can't be unsaid and actions can't be undone. For some, this practice might take time to develop but in the long run you'll be glad you did. It's far better to take the time to be sure you truly want to say what you originally want to, than to wish you hadn't!

Nobody is perfect, and there may be times you make a mistake when dealing with a customer. If you find yourself in this situation, apologize—IMMEDIATELY! Don't give a reason and don't try to make excuses. Just say you're sorry and ask them to forgive you. While they might not accept your apology, or forgive you, you must let it go and continue on as if the unpleasant situation hadn't occurred. Remember that the customer is always right, and do your best to meet their needs.

Section 2 | Developing Basic Skills

Customer feedback, whether positive or negative, is really important for you to take into consideration. Quite often the things you hear from a customer are the things you need to know in order to grow. Their comments are a great source for determining the next steps in building your business, since their needs can provide you with the blueprint you need to improve.

> **People love to do business with people who care about them and take care of their needs.**

Remember that there are lots of companies and services out there for people to choose from. What will distinguish you is your attitude of service. People love to do business with people who care about them and take care of their needs. If you develop a reputation of causing problems with customers you won't have your job or business very long. But if you develop one of being customer-focused and customer-friendly, the sky is the limit.

One important thing that people forget is to let customers know that you care about them and their business. If you let that show in your voice and in your words, they'll hear it, they'll sense it, and they'll tend to be more forgiving. If you really don't care, then perhaps you should find work elsewhere.

TEAMWORK

Whether you're the newest employee, the owner of the company, or the job supervisor, you're part of a team. Your efforts contribute to the team's success and the financial well-being of the company. Although each individual is required to perform to his or her best ability, it's the total team performance that determines success or failure.

Your favorite football team won't ever win a game unless each player does his part rather than trying to do everything alone. There's a certain amount of interdependence required of all members of a team for any endeavor to succeed. Each team member is 100 percent responsible for their own performance, and at the same time must depend on the work or contribution of others for overall success.

> It's the total team performance that determines success or failure.

Teams either pull together or pull apart. When a team pulls apart, conflict and dissension can undermine self-confidence, disrupt concentration, and interfere with individual performance. A successful team leader makes sure each individual has the tools and the knowledge to do their part. The leader does their own part to set the example, and guides, pulls, and pushes the others towards the goal line.

The following will help you get your team to pull together:

- Set goals and encourage everyone to work toward achieving them.

- Help your team see the consequences of pulling apart—poor individual and team performances, unhappiness, conflict, and so forth. Explain how pulling together will help the team be more successful and help everyone reach the goal.

- Hold each individual responsible for promoting this pulling together attitude by supporting and encouraging them.

- Identify and address any problem employees that are hurting company morale or are poor team members.

As a leader, don't overlook your group as a source of information to improve the way your team works. Ask questions. Listen. Be open to feedback. Welcome new ideas. Above all, have the flexibility and willingness to change if there's a better alternative.

Empower people through teamwork. Don't be afraid to delegate responsibility to others. If you believe you have a great team, you should have confidence in the individuals to whom you delegate responsibility. You should be fiercely dedicated to your team. If you aren't, ask yourself why, and then build that team that you can be proud of and fiercely dedicated to.

TIME MANAGEMENT

Ask any group of people what they wish they had more of. Some people will say money, of course. Some will say a better house or a nice car. You'll also get various other answers but the number one answer, the one that crops up the most often is—**TIME.** Time can be wasted, spent foolishly, or invested wisely, but never stored up for future use.

Three key elements to managing your time are:

1. **Knowing how you want to spend your time.** What are your goals and number one priorities? This is important to know so you don't waste time on things that don't move you closer to your goals.

2. **Organizing your time and planning your schedule.** Once you know where you want to spend your time, map it out, and get it on a calendar. This one step can make all the difference in how effective you are in your career and your life.

3. **Staying on top of things.** Don't wait for issues to crop up before you take action—consider your alternatives and set your plans into operation in time to forestall problems.

> True multitasking does not exist—it's definitely not a time-saving technique.

There's no such thing as multitasking. True multitasking does not exist and it's definitely not a time-saving technique. You can learn to work on several different projects, but not at the same time! If you're reading your emails while talking to someone, you're not doing a good job at either. If someone tries to talk to you while you're reading a book, you can't do that and listen to them at the same time. You'd need to close your book, hear what they have to say, and then re-open your book and continue reading. You'd have worked on two tasks (reading your book and listening to someone) but not at the same time. You can't focus 100 percent of your energy on more than one thing at a time, and if you try to do so, none of them will get completed satisfactorily. Proper time management doesn't require you to split your time, concentration, and efforts.

Here are some true time-saving ideas and techniques:

- **Stay organized.** The biggest time-waster is not being able to find the information you need when you need it. Find the system that works best to keep you on track. For instance, keep things that are most important on your kitchen counter or your desk. Put the next most important items in a drawer. Pending matters can be placed in the appropriate file. Trash anything that's not necessary.

- **Use technology.** Set up a single place to keep track of contact information, files, appointments, meetings, and recreational activities. A smartphone or web-based calendar are both easy to use and easy to share. Make it easy for others to coordinate activities or set meetings with you by keeping everything in one place. With dozens of free or inexpensive options available, the amount of time and aggravation you can save by having information at your fingertips far exceeds the effort required to put it in. The key to success it to start with a simple system and then diligently use it for everything.

> Use technology to set up organized systems.

- **Build a time cushion into your plans.** You've made a dental appointment for Tuesday at 11 a.m. that's scheduled to last for about one hour. You mark it on your calendar and know that you must set aside one hour for the appointment—**WRONG!** There are other considerations too—preparing for the appointment and the drive time to and from the location are examples. Add this time into your appointment and then add in a little extra to take into account unforeseeable delays that might occur such as the dentist or hygienist running late, road construction, or a delay due to an accident or bad weather.

- **Make quick decisions on small matters.** Decisions take energy. Small decisions that have little lasting impact can usually be made quickly with confidence. Some decisions however, take a great deal of time because of their importance and complexity. Be cautious when making quick decisions on big matters and consider the ramifications. If you're pressed for time, it might be appropriate for you to get help from someone else who's qualified to make a decision of this type. It's always worth the time and effort to work through the details with someone that has experience before you make a big decision.

- **Manage your projects.** To help you manage large projects efficiently, break them down into smaller tasks and list them in the order in which they need to be completed. Assign deadlines to each one and set up a project file that will help you keep track of each step and how close you are to completion. Even in this electronic age, sometimes a paper system can help you better manage your projects. Use a folder. On the inside cover of the project file, write the following information in pencil:

  - Names, telephone numbers, and addresses of all people involved if applicable
  - Tasks to be completed
  - Deadlines for each week
  - Dates and locations for any meetings

  Keep everything related to the project in this file. As you progress, check off the completed tasks and note any modifications to your project schedule.

Section 2 | Developing Basic Skills

- **Manage your emails.** If you work with email you need to find a system to manage your emails or your inbox will get totally out of hand. Create an email folder for each month of the year. Only keep emails in your inbox if you are planning to work on them this month. Everything else should be moved into the folder for the month you will take care of it. At the beginning of each month go through the emails for that month, and move the ones you will work on into your inbox. The others get moved to the next month's folder.

    - Your inbox now contains only those emails you will be working on this month. Sort them with the most recent one on the bottom! Yes, this is annoying, and will motivate you to get through your emails so that you can get to work on the newest one.

    - If you're waiting on something in order to complete the email you're on, leave it in your inbox. If not, then delete it. If it contains an authorization, or something important that you might need to refer back to, then save it in a folder. Don't make too many folders or you won't remember where you filed something, and be sure to make one for your purchases so that you can easily locate your receipts.

    - Adjust your settings so that emails only download to your inbox every 30 minutes; incoming emails are a distraction and you want to be able to finish what you are working on before the next one comes in—if you don't you might find yourself in the middle of everything with nothing completed, or worse yet, making mistakes.

- **To-do lists are important in spite of everyone saying they keep getting interrupted and don't finish them.** The important point is that if you do get interrupted, you know what didn't get done, or where you left off. Keep a log of your daily activities to determine how you're spending your time. Keep it faithfully for at least three days. Log everything you do and remember that you want to avoid wasted motion and time. If you have something to do and can't get it done, plan to complete it the next day or at the next available opportunity. Never allow one missed item to cause a delay for the remainder of the day (like the domino effect). Continue through the day, get things done, and don't waste time!

> **If you don't manage your time, someone else will!**

Leave time for attention to family, social affairs, personal needs, and hobbies. You must determine the importance of different things as they relate to your job, your personal life, your overall sense of accomplishment, and your needs and self-satisfaction

If you don't manage your time, someone else will! Protect your free time—everyone needs down time, to relax, have fun and get re-energized. Be sure to allocate sufficient time to pursue your personal interests.

Conclusion

Remember that skills are learned. They take time to put into practice and make perfect.

As you become more aware of the basic skills you need to be good at what you do, you'll want to look for good examples. Make it a habit to watch successful people around you, read great books, attend seminars, look at best practices, and take some courses. Develop new skills and document them for your resume.

Being effective, efficient and productive isn't an option—it's essential. Leaders understand they must continually improve these skills throughout their lives and careers. Your ability to communicate effectively and manage yourself and your relationships with others will set the bar on your career and future success.

Notes

SECTION 3
RAISING YOUR GAME

Introduction

There's a huge difference between being an employee and being an employee who's respected and considered a leader. Just like there's a huge difference between being an owner and being the type of owner who's truly respected and appreciated by his or her employees. Whatever role you're in, you want to be the kind of leader people look to for help, encouragement, and solutions.

As you start to accumulate more and more responsibilities, you'll need to find a way to manage all of them efficiently. To be successful, your goal should be to achieve the most you can with the least amount of effort ….

Ways to Raise Your Game Included in This Section are:

80–20 Rule	34
Assuming Responsibility	36
Creativity	39
Decision Making	40
Managing Your Money	43
Methods of Learning	44
Mistakes	45
Peer Pressure	47
Problem Solving	48
Weaknesses	50

80–20 RULE—THE PARETO PRINCIPLE

In the early 1900's, an Italian economist by the name of Vilfredo Pareto created a mathematical formula describing the unequal distribution of wealth he observed and measured in his country: Pareto observed that roughly twenty percent of the people controlled or owned eighty percent of the wealth. An avid gardener, he noticed that 80 percent of the yield of his pea crop came from 20 percent of the pea pods. He then noticed that the same ratio appeared in the distribution of land in Italy, where 80 percent of it was owned by 20 percent of the population. He observed that this was a pattern in many other situations as well.

> What 20 percent of your efforts are generating 80 percent of your results?

His observations laid the groundwork for what's known today as the Pareto Principle. In 1937, Dr. Juran, Quality Management pioneer, applied Pareto's observations about economics to a broader body of work. As a result, Dr. Juran's observation of the "vital few and trivial many," the principle that 80 percent of the effects come from 20 percent of the causes, became known as Pareto's Principle or the 80–20 Rule.

The impact of this rule can have large consequences for businesses and help leaders identify where they should focus their energy and their money—on the 20 percent that can have the most impact.

You can apply the 80–20 rule to your life and your career:

- What 20 percent of your team is generating 80 percent of the productivity?
- What 20 percent of your customers are generating 80 percent of your revenue?
- What 20 percent of your efforts are generating 80 percent of your results?

In fact, we can take it further:

Meetings—80 percent of the decisions come from 20 percent of the meeting time.

Time Management—80 percent of your measurable results/progress will come from just 20 percent of the items on your daily To-Do list.

Interruptions—80 percent of a leader's interruptions come from the same 20 percent of people.

Product Defects—80 percent of defects typically come from 20 percent of input errors.

Website—80 percent of your visitors will see only 20 percent of your website pages.

Advertising—20 percent of your advertising will produce 80 percent of your campaign's results.

When we look at it this way, it seems obvious that most of the effects (80 percent) come from the smallest number (20 percent) of causes.

The lesson here is for you to stop wasting precious time and resources on endeavors that drain money, energy, and time. Invest in the things that provide the largest return. The key is in how you evaluate the questions you might ask yourself such as:

- Do you want to reduce your living expenses? Identify which 20 percent are using 80 percent of the resources—carefully consider whether they're really necessary and get rid of them if they aren't. Take a bagged lunch to work rather than purchasing it; you'll be surprised at how much you're able to save in a short time.

- Do you have talented employees? Focus their energy in the areas that accomplish 80 percent of your goals, and be sure they're praised and rewarded for doing so.

- Are you having problems getting through your to-do list? If something's not going to get done make sure it's not part of that 20 percent!

> **Invest in the things that provide the largest return.**

Use of the Pareto Principle or "Pareto Thinking" should become a way of life for you. Your ability to separate the essential from the nonessential will improve with practice, especially if that practice involves use of actual data and not just "eye-balling" the situation. Once established, this approach becomes a normal reaction to solving problems. In time, an experienced "Pareto Thinker" can even make quick, accurate judgment calls.

ASSUMING RESPONSIBILITY

If you want to be successful you have to have the ability to assume responsibility and be open to taking ownership of new projects that come your way.

If a person is giving you a task, it clearly means they're confident in your ability to see it through to completion. They're trusting in you to figure it out and do it the best way you can. When a new task comes your way, you might not be that willing to take it on; it might even feel like an intrusion—you're already busy. However, part of growth and being good at your job is embracing new tasks and responsibilities and you need to realize that doing so shows a willingness to grow. Sometimes it can be uncomfortable and stressful, but if you work out how to get it done you'll feel a huge sense of accomplishment afterwards.

> Embracing new tasks and responsibilities shows a willingness to grow.

If something is assigned to you, it's yours 100 percent until completion. So what do you do? You already have 40 hours, and you feel like you have too much work. What you need to do is to review all of your current projects along with their priority and present the options to the person who assigned you the task so you can both agree as to how to move forward. Share your thoughts about various ways you can manage the time for the new project, such as:

1. Working overtime.
2. Not doing your other tasks.
3. Doing this new task and shifting your calendar out.
4. Assigning this task to someone else.
5. Putting this task further out on the calendar to do at a later time.

Once you're clear about the unfinished projects, and have discussed the options with the person who assigned you the task, then the decision can be made as to how to get it accomplished.

Once you've accepted responsibility for the task, and you're excited because you know you're valued, your focus will be on how to get it done. It's important that people working with you on other projects or people waiting on projects from you are aware of the consequences to them of this new project of yours.

1. Notify anyone who's waiting on you for something what the new completion date will be.
2. Find a way to streamline some of your tasks so they take less time allowing you to accomplish everything close to the original deadline.

Now what? You might feel overwhelmed and not know how to begin. You know you have to start somewhere, so just take a moment to think the project through and then start. If you hit a roadblock, go back to the person who gave you the task. Don't go to someone else for guidance because they may have no clue as to the goal or intended purpose so they might guide you down the wrong path. When you go to the person who gave you the assignment, they might realize they didn't make their goals clear or that you might not have understood how this project was to be used and they'll clarify things. It might even happen that when you re-discuss the goals and the purpose the whole nature of the project will be refined or changed. You might have to start all over again, but at least you'll know what the vision is.

> Make sure you understand the end goal and what you're trying to accomplish.

In order to do the task correctly, you need to understand the big picture. More importantly, you must understand its context. Make sure you understand the end goal and what you're trying to accomplish. Talk it through so you can be clear on your direction—ask questions so you know your destination. You might not be in a position where you can push back or doubt the person who gave you the project, but what should surface from the discussion is that there's agreement on its value, that it's worth pursuing, and also that it's part of the 20 percent you should be focusing on now.

Once that's established, you need to take control of the task until it's done:

- Identify the time frame for its completion.

- Find whether or not there's someone else on the team you're allowed to consult or work with.

- If there's a part of the task that requires someone else's input, be sure you include the person who assigned it to you when you email correspondence, so everyone is on the same page about where the project stands, and who the task is waiting on.

- If that other person can't get to their part immediately, then it's their responsibility to email back, with a copy to everyone, saying when they think they can get to it.

- Since the person who assigned you the task is copied on the correspondence, they have the option to say nothing and accept the schedule, or move priorities around to get it done sooner.

- If days or a week go by and you don't have what you're waiting for, send a reminder email, and copy the person who assigned the task to you. Remember it's still your responsibility to push the task to completion as quickly as possible, so you don't want it to fall off the radar. Everyone gets busy, and your boss might just assume it's been taken care of, when in fact it's waiting on someone other than you.

Section 3 | Raising Your Game

Take charge and proceed in a way that shows you have the vision and authorization to complete this project. If you need something from others, don't ask for permission just go and get it. Asking for permission is saying you don't believe that you're authorized to do so. If you need to ask for something because you need help, that's a different story—you should always ask for that. You've already been given the authorization, so do what it takes to get the job done.

> Growth doesn't come from being comfortable and inert.

Don't ask other people if they can do this for you because that just opens the door for a negative response. Tell them what you need to get done, and get their feedback on the best way to accomplish it. Be assertive in making sure the goal is met.

While you're working on the task, take full ownership of it by doing necessary research. Search the internet and learn everything you can about this topic. By seeing how others approach it you can increase your odds of doing an exceptional job on what's been assigned to you. You might see an opportunity for a new idea that didn't even present itself initially. What a picture of success that would be! Now you'll become the expert in whatever it is you were tasked with.

Always be willing to accept new tasks. Invite them! Sure, you may make mistakes, but embrace that fact as a part of your growth. Growth doesn't come from remaining comfortable or inert.

Remember, there's no such thing as inactivity unless you're planning on being out of a job or going out of business! Accept responsibility for the tasks that are assigned to you and make adjustments in your attitude or workflow to accommodate them. Change means you're growing and that you've tried something. The truly successful person who cares about their career will be open to new tasks and expanding responsibilities—this shows they care about their future and the business that hired them. Think about how great it will feel to know that you've significantly contributed to the company's success by your willingness to keep growing and finding ways to add value.

A word of caution. If you have skills and knowledge and keep accepting responsibility, you can fail miserably! You can fail if you assume too much. You will become overwhelmed, you'll start dropping the ball, making mistakes, omitting the small details and missing deadlines. You must learn when to push back and say you can't take in on at all, you can't take it on now, or you can do it, but at a later time. If you assume a responsibility, then along with that comes the need to know how and what to delegate from your current tasks the things that you don't need to be doing personally. That way, you can deliver what you commit to.

CREATIVITY

Always strive to be one step ahead of others by thinking of creative and innovative ways to accomplish your goals. You won't reach your full potential if you continue doing things the same old way. "We've always done it this way" is not an ingredient for success! Success depends on a good supply of timely information and creativity.

> Don't be afraid to try new things and go beyond what you're used to.

The world and technology are advancing so quickly that you need to be creative and innovative so that you don't get left behind. Innovation creates new or increased profits for your business or result in a reduction of man-hours and resources required to get the job done. Just as you strive to stand out in a crowd, so should your work. The way you approach a project, the way you communicate your ideas and the way you implement those ideas should stand out from others.

- Don't be afraid to try new things and go beyond what you're used to.
- Take chances and accept that there's a possibility of failure. Evaluate the risks involved and the consequences of taking those risks.
- Think outside of the box, expand your way of thinking and try new things.
- Look for inspiration by adapting to things that already exist. Watch other people. See what they buy, read, and wear. Be aware of the latest trends, whether or not they relate directly to what you do and see how you can adapt it in creative ways.
- Spend time on the internet searching for products and services, and advertisements that grab your attention and touch you emotionally. Always look for an aspect that you think is relevant and develop or adapt it for yourself or your company. Innovate on the success of others in creative ways.
- Read books about successful ideas and techniques used by others. Try them out!

Step out of your comfort zone. If you don't know if an idea will work—try it! Then you'll know for sure… True leaders reach great heights by utilizing innovative methods. Expand your thinking. Stretch your ideas and embrace new experiences.

DECISION MAKING

One of the first things you'll notice when you start to be seen as a leader is that you'll be constantly asked to make decisions. That can be one of the hardest responsibilities to accept—so much responsibility resting on your shoulders. Some decisions might be easy while others will have tremendous implications and consequences. In general, the bigger the consequence or financial magnitude, the more thought you should put into decision-making process. You'll want to consult with others, ask experts, and use all the resources you have available so you can make an informed decision.

Not every decision should be approached the same way, and so when you need to make one you should first ask yourself:

1. **Is it important?** What's the expected impact of the decision? Some decisions have very little effect on your company or yourself. Identifying early on how important a decision is allows you to bring the proper focus and energy to making it.

2. **Are you the right person to make the decision?** People will often come to you and ask you to make a decision for them. Ask yourself if you're the best person to answer their question, or if you should help them identify a path for themselves. Maybe someone else should make this decision now and in the future.

3. **Is it life-changing?** Ask yourself, "Is this decision a hair-cut or a tattoo?" Meaning, is this something that will be permanent or something that's short-term? Obviously long-term decisions require more thought, energy, and processing time than something that will be short-lived.

> The bigger the consequence, the more thought you should put into the decision-making process.

In every case, you need to consider all of your alternatives before making a decision. Don't close your mind to a single point of view. Listen to others first. Get honest feedback, gather all the information possible, and push back until you completely understand the situation and the consequences of the decision you're considering. Emotions, moods, and snap judgments are bound to influence you. Your final decision must be based on a clear and careful review of the situation, and the correct evaluation of the conditions, tempered by special circumstances, timing, and priorities. Then, a plan of action must be developed and put into place. Yes, it can be a complex and difficult undertaking! Don't make decisions under pressure.

Thinking on your feet. Sometimes it might be necessary and advantageous for you to "think on your feet" and make a decision in an instant that could greatly impact you and those around you. Initially this might make you uncomfortable, but remember that developing self-confidence comes from experience, preparation, and understanding the consequences of your decisions. That confidence is built using many small parts, such as reading, continuing education, learning from past decisions, and taking control of your emotions. The foundation of confidence is past success.

It's very important for you to pay full attention when being asked to make a decision. If you're only half listening because you're trying to read your email, or trying to finish up on another project, you'll only absorb part of what's being said and so will only have part of the information, reasoning, and facts. You'll only achieve part of what you should have and you'll make bad decisions.

Being consistent. A big part of the decision-making process is training the people around you on the factors that you consider while making your decisions. It's really important to create systems for the decision-making process for any project, and especially for those that are repeated. These systems will establish how to gather and present facts and how to look at them systematically. This not only encourages consistency, but also allows your employees or others on the team to grow and to learn to make the same quality decisions you would make whether you're there or not. For example, if you have a system, or a formula that you use as a basis for making a decision about ordering books or supplies, then the person responsible for presenting it to you for your approval should always use the same formula to come up with their proposal. If you do the research and perform the calculations the same way every time, then you'll know what you're saying yes or no to. You can always say, "Let's do 80 percent." Or, "Let's do 110 percent." based on current circumstances or compelling reasons, but your decision will be sound—for that moment!

> If you create decision-making models you'll reduce the need to constantly make new decisions!

Change. If you're being asked to make a decision on something that involves a change from what was done before, ask for the compelling reason for the change. What will you accomplish by making it? If there's no compelling reason, there's no reason to make the change. It's very easy to say yes to every request, and then as the years go by, and you look back at the evolution of that project, department, or product you might find yourself completely off track from your original goals and not understand quite how you got there. Keep your long-range goals in mind when you make decisions, and if it's not necessary to change what you've done in the past then don't do it. Go back and look at what you did the last time, so the good stuff isn't overlooked. If something worked, do it again. Ask yourself if making a change is going to result in something better. If not, continue doing it the same way. Of course, doing something the same way for years is no reason for you to continue doing it just because you've always done it that way. Decide on making a change after you've determined the compelling reason for it. If you create decision-making models you'll reduce the need to constantly make new decisions! Your decisions can be based simply on the new facts, rather than worrying about what else might have changed that you're not considering.

Section 3 | Raising Your Game

Having to make so many decisions can be overwhelming, so you'll need to find your stride. Confidence will come from experience. Also remember that being patient about making a decision is different than being indecisive. Sometimes it's better to just let the situation play out; it will either resolve itself, or the decision will make itself obvious in time.

> **Being patient about making a decision is different than being indecisive.**

I have a rule—there's so much information coming in at me, and so many decisions I'm asked to make, that if it's about something that's going to happen in the future, I don't even want to hear about it now. Don't tell me, because we won't discuss it. It fills my head, distracts me from what I need to concentrate on, and there's nothing I can do about it now anyway.

Move what's not important out to a future date and concentrate on the decision at hand. Slow down. Focus. Apply the 80–20 Rule.

MANAGING YOUR MONEY

Managing your money is also part of being a great leader. Many of the decisions that you will have to make as a leader will involve money. Whether it's a project that has to be within a budget or a wise purchase that makes your dollar go far, managing money is an important skill to have. You will constantly be faced with questions regarding money. As an owner, some of those questions might be: Can you buy the tool that you need to do the job? Can you afford to take the job? Can you afford the team that you need to do the work? Will doing the job result in you losing money?

Success with managing money on the job begins with how well you manage money in your personal life. Did you know that some employers run a credit check on you as part of their hiring process? If you can't manage your own money it will be impossible to manage the money of others. Personal financial management influences how you run your business. If you are in debt or have financial troubles this fear and money pressure can lead you to make poor long-term decisions and you may take unnecessary risks because you are under so much pressure. Don't Impulse-buy and take time to consider all purchases before committing.

> Personal financial management influences your business decisions.

Your objective should be to learn how to build a life based on the income that you have; to make a decision to save a certain amount each month and to get debt-free. Once you've achieved financial freedom, your life will be significantly different. You'll be able to weigh future options and make sound decisions without being swayed emotionally by your financial concerns, which is what happens when you have stress that's related to not having enough money. The day you become debt-free you will have stability and security and this will open up new opportunities and flexible ways to approach your work and your personal life.

Your personal financial freedom should be your first goal on your step to financial leadership, and when you understand the process, it will become the model for your professional life. There are many books and programs on the market that can get you started on the right track and instruct you on how to become financially free; Dave Ramsey is just one author who has a complete program that teaches you to *Take Control of Your Money*. This process of training yourself for financial success will carry over to all the other areas of your life. At the end of the day, true leaders have control over all areas of their business and their lives, especially their finances.

METHODS OF LEARNING

There are differences in the way people learn just as there are differences in the way they communicate. In order to improve your ability to teach or lead it's essential for you to be aware of how you yourself learn and also how those around you do. Being cognizant of how people learn has an effect on staffing, training programs, project schedules, and the ability to meet deadlines.

Most people are visual learners, some are auditory learners, and a few are tactile/kinesthetic learners.

Visual learners think in pictures and learn best from visual displays.

Auditory learners learn best through verbal lectures, discussions, and listening to what others have to say.

Tactile/kinesthetic learners are people who learn best through a hands-on approach; moving, doing, and touching.

Some individuals may learn best by having someone communicate information verbally in a step-by-step manner, while others might learn best by observing someone demonstrating what needs to be done. Some individuals may learn best by experimenting on their own without the interference of anyone's demonstration or verbal instruction. To be an effective trainer you need to be sure you recognize and understand these different learning styles. You can begin to recognize the differences by listening and observing responses to your attempts at communication. "I hear, and I imagine"; "I see, and I understand"; "I do, and I remember forever!"

> If you find that the person isn't learning, try a different approach.

If you're teaching someone how to complete a task be sure you're detailed and break it down step-by-step. Take the time to be sure you were understood by asking questions or having them repeat what you've said. Clearly answer any questions they might ask without being sarcastic or cynical. Remember that there's really no such thing as a stupid question! If you find that the person you're teaching isn't learning or responding in the way you expected them to, then perhaps you need to try a different approach.

To be an effective leader you need to be an effective trainer. You should be able to recognize how the members of your team learn, and be able to use different teaching styles that are suited to their individual needs.

MISTAKES

We all make mistakes so join the crowd—you're in good company! Thomas Edison's teachers said he was "too stupid to learn anything." He was fired from his first two jobs for being nonproductive and made 1,000 unsuccessful attempts at inventing the light bulb. Did you know that Abraham Lincoln went to war as a captain and managed to finish as a private? Talk about mistakes! Consider Henry Ford's words the next time you make a mistake and feel like a failure, "Failure provides the opportunity to begin again, more intelligently."

Mistakes sometimes make us feel like a failure or appear foolish or incompetent. Here are three steps to take to help you bounce back after a mistake:

1. **Learn the lesson.** Any thoughts about a mistake made should focus on how to learn from it. What was controllable? What will you do if the situation arises in the future? How can anyone else learn from your mistake? In other words, accept the responsibility for your decision that led to the mistake, learn from it, and then move on.

2. **Avoid dwelling on a mistake**; remind yourself that we all make them. By not dwelling on a mistake it's easier to set it aside and just let it go. Once you've made a mistake, there's no way to go back in time and do or say things differently. It's done. Going over it again and again serves no useful purpose. In fact doing so can lead to self-directed anger or increased embarrassment.

3. **Create a positive mental setting** for the rest of your tasks. Positive focus gives you the ability to change the direction of your energy instead of continuing to make mistakes because you're upset. Remind yourself that you've been successful many times before—and will be again! Focus on what good performance looks like.

> Be open-minded about mistakes and realize that they're going to happen – it's what we learn from them that counts.

Whether the mistake is yours or someone else's, don't aggravate the issue by asking: "Why did you do such a stupid thing?" but rather ask, "How can we correct this?" File it away immediately. If further analysis is necessary, it should be done at a later time, after the immediate negative impacts have lost their edge.

Many people aren't willing to accept responsibility for a mistake and tend to "blame" others, possibly erroneously. Any "blame" for a mistake should always be focused on a controllable aspect of the situation (you should have made sure the circuit was turned off) rather than a personal weakness you might think you have (I'm stupid). Be open-minded about mistakes and realize that they're going to happen – it's what we learn from them that counts.

Section 3 | Raising Your Game

We all have "bad" days and "good" days—it happens. One of the most important things to learn to do is to develop a positive attitude, especially when it seems the most difficult. No one really intends to go out and make mistakes. If you don't know that you have to do something, or if you haven't been properly trained to do something, you might make a mistake by not doing it.

> **Mistakes that happen because someone doesn't care aren't that forgivable.**

Mistakes that happen because of a lack of information or a lack of correct information are part of the learning process. Mistakes that happen because someone **doesn't care** aren't that forgivable. They might be excused or tolerated once or twice, but there should be no place in your business or on your team for those that don't care. No matter how hard we might try, or how well-planned a process may be, people are human, mistakes are made, and consequences exist. Join Thomas Edison, Abraham Lincoln, and Henry Ford in recognizing that mistakes are opportunities to LEARN.

PEER PRESSURE

When we think of "peer pressure" we think about parents being concerned about their children following the example of the "wrong" type of crowd, the use of drugs, underage drinking, and so on. However, it isn't just children and teens who succumb to peer pressure. It can affect anyone of any age because we all want to be accepted, to be part of a group we admire, and we're afraid of being "different."

People have a natural tendency to conform; they don't want to stand out, or they want to be accepted, so they listen to their friends, co-workers, and associates. Unfortunately, people around you don't always support your goals or don't have goals of their own. They may put down your aspirations for a variety of reasons. If you're trying to better yourself, perhaps by going back to college, chances are good that someone is going to make fun of you because they feel threatened by your goals.

It's unfortunate but true—many people like to make others feel stupid. Putting someone down is somehow easier than building them up. Opinions and recommendations are often given without knowing the facts. Sadly, there are far too many people who don't like to see others become successful.

Everyone wants to feel accepted and, unfortunately, many times we adjust our behavior and attitudes to match those of the majority, giving little consideration to our own feelings. If it doesn't feel right, then it's wrong. Resist making decisions based on what other people do or feel unless it's something with which you agree. For instance, if you'd rather work in a rural area where most of the jobs are residential, don't go to work for an electrical contractor who only does commercial work in large cities, merely because "everyone" says you can make more money doing so. You'll find yourself becoming unhappy and less productive which can have a negative impact on your image and self-esteem.

> If it doesn't feel right, then it's wrong.

Assess your own strengths and limitations objectively. Make your decisions and perform your activities based on your own knowledge and ability. If you choose to take someone's advice and accept their opinions, do so with an open mind. A bit of old-time wisdom fits in here very appropriately—"To thine own self be true." If you do so you usually can't go wrong!

PROBLEM SOLVING

Problems are encountered every day—at home, at work, with our families, and with our friends and associates. We spend a tremendous amount of time and energy trying to solve them.

The key to effective problem-solving is to:

1. Identify the problem.
2. Gather facts.
3. Identify all possible solutions.
4. Evaluate the effectiveness of all solutions.
5. Make the best decision possible at that time.
6. Analyze whether it impacts anything else in the company or your life that may need to be adjusted to avoid this problem in the future.
7. Learn from the process and you'll become a better problem solver.

It's impossible to anticipate every possible problem, even with the most careful planning. You can't accurately predict long-range weather, sickness, or business conditions that might have an effect on whether or not you have a job. So, when a problem shows up, make sure you understand the facts in order to deal with it directly. Dealing with the side effects or secondary impacts won't remove it.

Some companies use meetings to solve problems that happen in the workplace, but quite often they're not the most effective venues for doing so. Very often meetings end up being attempts to assign blame. Participants take turns pointing fingers at someone else because they're focusing on the details of the problem. One way to make problem-solving more effective during meetings is to ask everyone, at the beginning, to discuss the meeting's purpose and to ask them to focus on solutions rather than the assignment of blame.

> "Don't bring me problems, bring me solutions!"

Encourage the people around you to think through the problem before bringing it to you to solve for them. Let them formulate a few of their own solutions that they can present to you as options. You might choose one of them, which will validate their efforts. On the other hand, you might have one of your own that's better, in which case that person will have broadened their perspective and do better the next time. I use that technique with my employees and it seems to work very well because it not only reduces my problem-solving responsibilities, but it instills greater confidence in problem solving for them. I tell them—"Don't bring me problems, bring me solutions! I have more than enough problems—what I need are solutions for the ones I already have!"

Effective problem solving is a critical component to effective leadership. Make it a practice to pay close attention to how others solve problems and be open to what's being said and done. Get in the habit of looking into the reasons the problems occurred, and use them as a building block to improve. If there were no problems, failures, or shortcomings in technology, some of the greatest innovations might never have happened. In many situations creativity is a response to a problem.

> In many situations creativity is a response to a problem.

WEAKNESSES

> Think of your own weaknesses as challenges and work to overcome them.

Everyone has weaknesses. You might think of your own weaknesses as challenges, since that implies you can work on them to overcome them. It's extremely important for you to objectively analyze your weaknesses so you can determine how you can rise above them.

We'll only talk about a few here to give you some ideas of how to come up with alternative or corrective measures you can apply.

Weakness: Immaturity.

Solution: If others have told you that you're immature, get more facts from them. Try to understand the areas in which you're immature, and work hard to develop maturity and improve your problem-solving and decision-making skills. Doing so will increase your self-confidence.

Weakness: Temperamental.

Solution: Everyone gets angry and gets their feelings hurt, but what's important is how you handle it. Make a concerted effort not to allow personal problems or feelings to affect your decisions or your performance. Learn to develop patience and to not take things so personally. Others might have their own problems and could be acting out for reasons that have nothing to do with you. You have a responsibility to others to control your emotions.

Weakness: Can't handle criticism.

Solution: Criticism given improperly often feels like a personal attack and results in hard feelings and diminished self-confidence. Consider the person offering the advice. If you know the individual is concerned about you, try to accept this constructive criticism graciously. Be open to self-improvement. What they're saying about you is either true and is an area you need to develop, or it isn't so you don't need to worry about it. Criticism is often the fuel to help you get to the next level.

Weakness: Perfectionist.

Solution: Perfection is an elusive quality and a real stress inducer. Trying to be perfect will overwhelm you to the point you won't get anything done. Strive for great, not perfect. Expecting perfection in others is to set yourself up for failure. Understand that in most cases everyone is doing the best they can. Even if you can change, don't expect it of others. Be fair and realistic in your dealings with everyone.

Weakness: Poor communicator.

Solution: Make sure that when you have written communication you use the spell-checkers and grammar checkers that are provided with software. Bad spelling doesn't make a good impression. If you know that you make mistakes when you talk because your language and grammar in school weren't your focus points, make an effort to take a class or read so that you can improve in this area. The language you use when you talk sends a message.

There are obviously many more things that can be considered weaknesses, or personal challenges to overcome. Take some time to make an objective list of those areas in which you feel you can improve. Try to think of strategies or solutions. Be careful when you ask others what your weaknesses are—you might receive more frankness than you anticipated. Be prepared to handle it and learn from it.

> **Make an objective list of those areas in which you feel you can improve.**

Section 3 | Raising Your Game

Conclusion

Life is a continuous process of raising your game. When you bring creativity, the right attitude, a spirit of learning and laser-like focus to the way you approach your life, you can't help but achieve success.

To maximize your personal productivity and raise your game, use the Pareto Principle and realize that of the many things you do during your day, only 20 percent really matter! Identify and focus on those things. What do you do with those that are left over? Either delegate them or don't do them.

Work Smart—identify your 20 percent now!

SECTION 4
DEVELOPING OTHERS

Introduction

As an individual you can never grow if you always choose to do everything yourself.

As a leader, your job is to give your team the tools they need to operate at 100 percent of their capacity, to accept 100 percent responsibility for what they do, and to encourage them to reach their peak performance. Coaching and training others isn't only rewarding, it's always an effective strategy to improve your ability to make a difference in your business and your personal life.

Even if you're not the owner of your company, you can still help others develop their skills by sharing things that have been effective in your life, and by being a great example. Don't be afraid to share what you know—you'll be surprised at how much you get back, and how much you'll grow yourself!

Great Tips to Develop Others Include:

> Choosing Your Management Style 54
> Delegation. 56
> Instilling Confidence in Others 59
> Management by Crisis. 60
> Motivation. 61

Section 4 | Developing Others

CHOOSING YOUR MANAGEMENT STYLE

> Your management style is strongly influenced by your own self-confidence.

Your leadership or management style is strongly influenced by your own self-confidence and by how you make decisions and relate to the people around you. It's also strongly influenced by your beliefs and assumptions about what motivates people.

"Theory X" and "Theory Y" were created and developed by Douglas McGregor at the MIT Sloan School of Management in the 1960s.

Theory X stresses the importance of strict supervision and external rewards and penalties. If you believe that employees dislike work, you'll tend towards using this authoritarian style of management. It assumes that:

- Most people dislike work and will avoid it when they can.
- People must be pushed and threatened with punishment in order to get them to produce enough to achieve objectives.
- The average person has very little ambition, wants to be directed, and will avoid responsibility whenever possible.
- Life isn't fair; rewards don't follow results.
- Leaders must do all of the planning for the team.

Theory Y highlights the motivating role of job satisfaction and allows workers to approach tasks creatively. If you assume that employees take pride in doing a good job, you'll tend to adopt this more participative style. It assumes that:

- People naturally want to work, as children want to play.
- People will manage themselves in order to achieve goals they set for themselves.
- Peoples' level of commitment to goals and objectives is related to the rewards for the achievement of them.
- Under the proper conditions, people will learn to accept and seek out responsibilities.
- The ability to imagine, demonstrate ingenuity, be creative, and to develop solutions to problems is naturally shared by most people to some degree.
- People want to participate in planning their own future.
- People want to contribute to the highest degree they can.
- People believe that rewards follow results, that the game is fair.
- Leaders should only review plans that have been developed in collaboration with the team, not totally develop the plan for it.

Re-read the previous statements and make a note of which ones you agree with, and which ones you don't. You might be surprised— but your beliefs will affect how you interact with the people on your team, and those that you lead.

The finding is that managers who tend toward Theory X may be effective short-term, but won't be successful in the long run. By always creating tension and competition, you inject an element of fear which might result in pulling the team apart instead of keeping them together and working toward a common goal. Managers who employ Theory Y will allow their team to learn and grow, and as a result produce better performance and results. In order to achieve long-term success, you need a team of people who want to be at work and want to do good work— together. The key to Theory Y's success is in building commitment through great communication, clearly stated goals, and a strong relationship with your team or your employees.

> Determine how you can use your traits to be effective with people around you.

Since not everyone responds to learning or direction in the same way, many managers find themselves employing a combination of styles based on the dynamics of the group, the type of work being done, the types of decisions that need to be made, and the deadline for completion of the work.

The mold of a good leader isn't cast from one personality type. Some people are naturally bold, brash, dominating, on-their-feet thinkers, and are quick to give orders or make decisions. Others are silently strong, careful, thoughtful, considerate, not taking risks but always choosing the safe, solid path. Both styles will win and lose in a given number of circumstances; both will produce results, but at very different paces and with different consequences. Whatever your personality type, you need to determine how you can use your traits (both positive and negative) to be effective with the people around you, set the tone, and create an atmosphere of commitment.

Some managers might confuse management with power. Being an effective manager isn't about enforcing your will on others; it's not about control or influence over your team by virtue of your position. If you're a good manager and leader, set a good example, are respected, open and approachable, you'll have natural power.

Get in the habit of observing the people with whom you associate regularly so you become familiar with their communication style, individual mannerisms, and their body language. You'll find that the more you understand them, the more things will be accomplished without misunderstanding—and be especially aware and respectful of cultural differences.

DELEGATION

As you progress along your career track, and your life, it's important for you to become a great delegator so you can get more accomplished yourself. That means you'll have to task someone else with doing something that you used to do yourself. As a manager or team leader, you'll need to know how to determine the strengths of your team members so you'll know the most effective way to match the task to the person. If you aren't able to delegate effectively, then you won't be able to lead properly or manage others competently, and you'll certainly restrict the opportunities for growth that might otherwise become available.

Ask any new manager what the hardest thing is they need to learn, and they'll tell you that learning to delegate is close to the top! When you're used to doing something, and of course you believe you're the best for that task, it's hard to give it up. Will it be done right? What if a mistake is made? What if something isn't done because they just didn't know they needed to do it? All of your own experience and processes in your brain guide you and trigger reminders, but when you delegate, you lose control of this. This fear of losing control of all of the aspects of a task from A to Z (micromanagement) is what leads to the failure of some managers, and prevents them from growing into leaders.

> The key to being successful is in how you train your team and hand off tasks.

The key to being a successful delegator is in how you train your team and hand off tasks. Consider each person's role, level of pay, and contribution to the team. Be sure they understand not only the role they're currently playing, but what success looks like. It's a common misconception that practice makes perfect—it doesn't! Practice only promotes familiarity—practice makes permanent! To improve through practice, you must study and analyze your performance during practice, and then improve on your past performance.

Before you can delegate a specific job to another individual and let go of the responsibility, you'll need to train them to do it. Make sure they understand the goals and the vision. Make sure you take the time to show them your process and how you make your own decisions. If you happen to not be available when a decision needs to be made, and you've taught your process to your team, then they'll know how to make it themselves. You want the business to be able to be maintained in your absence, with the same spirit and values as if you were there.

Letting go can be difficult, but the key is to know that you've done your part by training them correctly. Let them know you believe they can handle the job and that you're available to help if they run into trouble. Training builds confidence and various tasks become second nature. Delegation doesn't mean you give up responsibility and control. You should continue to provide input in a timely fashion, but only when the need arises. When you're delegating, it's okay to include your recommendations, but remember to leave that person some creative space too. Monitor their progress without appearing to hover over their shoulders.

It goes without saying that effective delegation requires clear communication. If those points are understood, the delegation will prove to be successful.

1. **Clearly Explain How the End Result Should Look.** Spell out the details, deadlines, and objectives and explain why the task might need to be performed in a specific sequence and manner. If possible give a model, or an example.

2. **Explain Why the Project is Important and How it Fits Into Overall Goals.** Success involves understanding the objectives to be achieved, and the resources that are available.

3. **Make Sure They're Trained.** If the task is something they've never done, you'll probably need to tell them how to do it and then be sure it's done properly, but you shouldn't need to do so more than once or twice.

4. **Put it in Writing.** The task might initially be overwhelming. Notes will provide clarity and a point of reference.

> Effective delegation requires clear communication.

5. **Check in Fairly Quickly to be Sure They're on the Right Track.** Once your team has started a task, check in after a few minutes to see how they're doing. This will give you the opportunity to be sure it's being completed properly and to correct them if it isn't—before the project is complete. It's much easier to fix something early on than it is to redo the task.

6. **Set a Deadline.** Everyone works better if they know how much time they have to complete a task.

7. **Let the Person Put Their Own Spin on it.** As long as the final result is what you defined, and the person knows that he or she has the authority and responsibility to perform the task, you shouldn't be telling them how to do it, or standing over them while they do it. Each person's creativity and input should be allowed to come through.

8. **Handle Any Resistance.** Find out what's really going on. If you see any struggle or conflict, check to see if it's fear, or lack of knowledge about a particular part of the project. Explain the project again to make sure a lack of understanding isn't the problem.

9. **Give Lots of Credit When the Project is Completed.** Praising the people responsible for a task well done validates their efforts.

10. **If There's a Failure.** If the project misses it's deadline, or wasn't completed as planned, analyze the situation to determine if you were the problem; learn from the issues, and if your decision was at least partly the cause, improve your methods of delegating. Remember, it's not necessary or professional to publicly discuss any problems or errors that have been made. Corrections, directions, and constructive criticism should be made privately in a conversation between the two people involved. In regard to criticism (whether giving or receiving), the way you react to it will be remembered more vividly than the argument you present. Raising your voice or using inflammatory language should never be done. These reactions hurt your chance for future effective communication.

11. **Start Small and Leave Room for Errors.** Make sure everyone knows what you expect of them and encourage them to approach you if they have too much or too little to do. That way tasks can be reassigned or new ones created by you delegating additional projects. Urge your team to take advantage of any downtime between tasks or jobs by thinking about ways in which they might be able to improve the process. You might not be managing your projects properly if you find that they do in fact, have too much downtime. Pay attention to the smallest details, and use them to help grow the organization.

> Training is important; but what occurs after training is even more important.

It's true that what occurs during training is important; but what occurs after training is even more important. Training attempts to change something. Leaders must know what was covered during a training program and follow up to ensure the training is being applied; that is, that the desired change has occurred. If not, the training activity failed or the trainee failed the true training test.

Effective delegation is one of your most important leadership skills. You can improve morale, increase productivity (your own and others), and ease the stresses of your job and life—**if** you delegate wisely.

INSTILLING CONFIDENCE IN OTHERS

Actual performance is directly related to an individual's feeling of competence and expectations of personal effectiveness. To be a good leader, you have the opportunity to help others gain greater self-confidence. Keep track of the positive accomplishments of your group and remind them of their growth. The purpose of these reminders is to continually acknowledge how far they've grown and developed, and what they can reasonably expect of themselves in the future. Help the people around you visualize what they're capable of.

> Help the people around you visualize what they're capable of.

Remind them of what it feels like to perform well, and realistically explain where they stand in terms of what they're capable of today. This kind of attention will foster the self-confidence necessary for people to demonstrate their capabilities again and again. Be careful not to raise expectations to a level they can't possibly achieve. Reflect for a moment on the following points:

- Personal excellence is largely a matter of believing in one's capabilities and performing with a sense of pride, perseverance, and commitment to identified objectives.

- Self-esteem is the strength of one's convictions that they can successfully execute the behavior/actions required to produce a certain outcome.

- Expectations and potential rewards determine how much effort people expend and how long they'll persist in the face of adversity.

It's well worth your effort to concentrate on these areas of development. Remember—first you build your team up; then you must motivate them with the positive accomplishments you see them achieving. The task is never finished.

Section 4 | Developing Others

MANAGEMENT BY CRISIS

To avoid working or living in an atmosphere of constant crisis, urgent deadlines, perpetual emergencies, and never-ending changes in priorities, pay attention to what you're doing and how you're managing your schedule and your projects!

Perpetual management by crisis occurs when there's no vision, and no clearly stated goals or systems in place to move your business or career forward. If all of your time is taken up putting out fires, or reacting to problems and not initiating positive action, then you have an atmosphere of continuous crisis that will wear you down and create negative stress. When your team isn't properly trained, when you're disorganized, or when you don't have a plan, you'll feel like you're spending most of your time managing crises.

> **Perpetual management by crisis occurs when there's no vision.**

Obviously, effective crisis management is a great skill to have. The unexpected will always happen, especially when you don't expect it! You'll need to be able to switch lanes, re-assign tasks, react quickly, and move to solve the problem. However, this should only be needed in true times of crisis or occasional problems. It becomes a real issue when you're the source of the problem and your lack of leadership is what's causing repeated crisis within the company. When there's no control and no planning, the result is a growth (in epidemic proportion) in negative stress.

Work off your goals, manage your time, set priorities, train your team, delegate effectively and you'll eliminate the stress involved with chronic crisis, and then you'll have the energy to effectively manage your business during true and unexpected times of real crises.

Remember:

- Chronic crisis management occurs when there's no planning.
- Eliminate those tasks that waste time or can be delegated to someone else.
- Know what you have to do, plan your course of action, and do it—now!
- Complete all tasks in their order of priority.

MOTIVATION

Before you can motivate others, you must first be motivated yourself. You need to have a firm understanding of where you're going and know your overall vision of success. If you're aggressive about accomplishing your goals and excited about taking on the challenge, you'll motivate others by your example. You must share your vision and your goals with your team so they can also see the big picture. Your job is to lift them out of mediocrity and help them become achievers.

Motivating others is extremely important. Unmotivated people can affect more than you might think at first. When you're on the job, a lack of motivation can have an adverse effect on the customer, create friction on the project, result in substandard output in quality, and in people quitting, being late, or just plain not showing up. All of these factors affect everyone around you. It's a fact that motivated people are the most productive and will produce to their maximum abilities while unmotivated people can bring the whole company down.

To bring about a positive change in the behavior of others, leaders need to be aware of, and deal with, the different motives people have for performing their tasks. This is the most critical ingredient to a successful formula for motivating people.

> It's a fact that motivated people are the most productive.

Leaders should provide the environment that supports achievement, sets the tone of expectation for success, and takes into consideration the incentives for action, which differ from individual to individual. There are, however, dangers in the use of external pressure on others to perform. If there's too much it can hamper their level of performance. You can increase internal motivation by including others while the company's goals and the vision are being drafted so you receive bigger buy-in and commitment from your team.

Learn how to ask questions **and then listen to the answers**. By asking questions your goal is to challenge the status quo, so the team can find ways to make things better. Encourage critical thinking, inspire other perspectives, and be willing to learn and change. You can learn to ask questions that don't intimidate or put the other person on the spot; questions that aren't threatening and will encourage dialogue such as, "Do you see any other ways to do this?" rather than "Why did you do it this way?" Ask, "How are you doing on the project?" instead of "Why aren't you finished?"

Section 4 | Developing Others

Stress the attainment of small goals. Self-confidence is built on accomplishments. Look for gradual gains. Know your group. What motivates one individual might have little or no effect on another. Any motivational strategy you use should have realistic and attainable goals toward which the whole group (and the individuals within the group) can strive.

> Self-confidence is built on accomplishment. Look for gradual gains.

Practice and teach self-reinforcement. Nurture an understanding in your team of their own capabilities; in other words, let them know their strengths and weaknesses. Establish two-way communication; instead of telling people what they did wrong and telling them to correct it, ask them what they thought they did wrong, and what they'll do differently next time. Two-way communication also results in better and more specific feedback, which enables people to improve more quickly.

Motivating others isn't a simple task. It's very difficult and requires significant skill to execute fairly. If you're not sincere, they'll sense it. If you lack genuine care for others, they'll find out. If you're manipulative, they'll become angry. Some people can mentor, some can lead, and some can do both. Know your own limits.

Conclusion

Don't overlook the people around you as a source of information to improve your own work.

Empower others through training and teamwork. Don't be afraid of delegating responsibility to others—it propels everyone, especially you, to greater heights. Don't think that developing others diminishes your role or importance. On the contrary, you'll never grow without competent people around you.

There's no one right way to do this. Do your research, read, and find a style that you can get behind and emulate.

Notes

SECTION 5
STAYING ON TOP OF YOUR GAME

Introduction

Being a leader doesn't have anything to do with your seniority in the chain of command, nor does it have anything to do with your title, or lack thereof. It has everything to do with your positive influence on the people around you for the greater good. Regardless of your position, you can command respect and be thought of as a leader.

Staying effective is as much of a challenge as getting there. It involves being aware of a changing environment, responding to the needs of others, being open to new ideas (including criticism), staying current, and (most importantly) taking care of yourself.

These Ways to Stay on Top Will be Discussed in This Section:

Burnout	66
Change	69
Continuous Education	71
Memberships	74
Procrastination	75
Stress Management	77

BURNOUT

At some point in our lives, each of us has felt like we were experiencing burnout. When you work hard, have commitments to others, and have big goals it can sometimes be a challenge to keep everything in balance.

A simplistic explanation of burnout is that it occurs when our work and the pressures of life have become so intense that there's a lack of motivation, or a "don't care" attitude about life. It involves psychological, emotional, and sometimes physical withdrawal from a formerly enjoyable activity.

> It can sometimes be a challenge to keep everything in balance.

Keep a watchful eye out for signs of "burnout" both in your life and the lives of your family members. It can occur during times of intense study and long working hours. If burnout is the result of a new project at work, or the time you're spending studying for an exam if you're in school, it's important to remind yourself and your family that it's temporary and is only for a relatively short period of time. Sometimes burnout happens because of life challenges. If you find yourself overwhelmed it's important to figure out what's making you feel that way and take direct steps to change how you approach work, personal responsibilities, or the intensity you place on your everyday challenges. Regardless of the reason, burnout is a real danger to your ability to manage the pressures of everything you have on your plate.

Sometimes, it's not easy to realize you're experiencing burnout. Jessica Stillman, (contributor, Inc.com) identified some of the signs in her article, 5 Surprising Signs of Burnout. They include:

Signs of Burnout

- Inability to concentrate
- Guilt
- Frequent mood changes
- Social isolation
- Increased use of alcohol, food, and/or drugs

Are You Experiencing Burnout?

- Do your spouse, children, or friends complain that you need to spend more time with them? Do they feel that they're last on the list for your time?

- Do you have many business associates, but few friends?

- Do you work even in nonworking situations?

- Do you work at your play? Is all your recreation as much work as being on the job because you play to win every point, improve every previous performance, and refuse to take losing lightly?

- Do you feel uncomfortable if you're in a situation where you can't be productive and grow nervous as you wait for things even so minor as a red light to change in traffic?

- Do you think of no goal-related fun as frivolous?

- Do you let the clock run your life?

- Do you take everything so seriously that you miss or resent humorous comments at home in a work situation?

Once you recognize the symptoms of burnout, take positive steps to counter its negative effects. Research the web for additional information and tools that will help you get through this difficult period. Evaluate situations objectively and then implement solutions. Perhaps this is the time for you to do more delegating both at home and work, even if only temporarily. Take some time to brainstorm solutions to all of the things weighing on your mind, and sometimes by just writing them down you'll find that they aren't as big as you've made them out to be..

> If you're starting to feel yourself becoming overwhelmed this is a huge red flag.

Avoiding Burnout

Take some time out—take a break! Force yourself to make time for yourself and your family. Turn off the cellphone, don't watch the news on TV, don't answer your emails, and disconnect from your daily chores and obligations. Do something that's totally different and that you find relaxing so you can give your mind and body a rest. You deserve it, and your family and friends deserve it. You should be determined to enjoy them every day—life is too short, and the unexpected happens. You want to be able to say you enjoyed all of your moments and not have regrets about not taking time or making time to relax and enjoy all of the wonderful things and people in your life.

Section 5 | Staying on Top of Your Game

Take your vacations regularly. Companies give paid vacation because they understand the need for people to have the time to rest and re-energize so they can continue to be productive. The same goes for your personal life. So if you're starting to feel yourself becoming overwhelmed this is a huge red flag that now is the time to take that time off and to step away. A vacation can just be a day! If you don't have the money, or really can't spare the time to take off for a week or more, you can just go away for a day… Go with your friends or family to your favorite fishing hole, or your favorite theme park—or go alone if that's what you really need! You can make a single day off (or two) be as special as you choose. You can't afford not to take time off and the relief you'll feel will make you that much more ready to face whatever it is when you return.

> Everyone needs to take time to relax and have fun.

A good antidote for burnout is to become involved with outside interests that you find relaxing—exercise, sports, social meetings, club memberships, and so on. Get away from your everyday responsibilities and relax and enhance your creativity. **Protect your free time!** Everyone needs to take time to relax and have fun. Engage in hobbies or other pursuits that you enjoy. Don't become a workaholic.

CHANGE

Be a person who embraces and thrives on change. No matter where you are in your career or personal life, one thing is certain—to be successful you need to be able to adapt to change. All of us are faced with change on a daily basis; very few things stay the same. Methods and techniques that worked in the past may not work today. Technological advances are occurring at such rapid and varying rates that methods, materials, and even tools that worked well in the past are becoming obsolete before they've had a chance to get worn out.

You must not only be aware of the changes that have an influence on you, you must also put yourself in a position to move forward and embrace them as soon as possible. You need to understand the inevitability of change and the necessity of growing with it in order to remain competitive. It's natural to resist change because it's easier to do things the same way you've always done them. Everyone has his or her own level of resistance to new things, but if you embrace change and consider it an opportunity to learn and grow, you'll find it much easier. Making necessary changes might be nothing more than practicing a new technique, or learning a new way of using a familiar tool.

Wanting to learn and staying abreast of new developments comes easier than **having** to do it. When you start something new, your ability to accept initial failures improves your chances of final success. One way to stay ahead and keep up with what's happening in your environment is to read trade publications, join associations, and attend meetings. Becoming involved and active will help you see upcoming changes and stay current.

> Embrace change and consider it an opportunity to learn and grow.

Technology is evolving almost faster than we can keep up with. Computers, laptops, smart phones, tablets, and other electronic devices have become a necessity where they used to be considered new or a luxury. This generation is growing up with advanced technology, but if you've been around a little while, it's important for you to have at least a basic knowledge of these tools. If you're running a business, commit to learning and using spreadsheet and word processing software as some of the tools to help you be effective. Spreadsheets are used for a variety of finance-related subjects and are often used to summarize information in the form of a table. In addition, learning how to type quickly is a big plus because it allows you to produce written communications more quickly. Investing your time in learning these skills can help you stay in the game. Make every effort to stay as current as possible with technological advances by searching the Internet for information about new technology—and then READ it! Challenge yourself to broaden your horizons, extend your personal knowledge, and always be willing to learn and grow.

Section 5 | Staying on Top of Your Game

It's vitally important for you to develop and maintain a sense of objectivity and a willingness to recognize change as an ever-present factor in your life. Change occurs from within as well as from the outside. Positive change can be brought about through implementation of your planned goals. Action and planning (not reaction to events) must be the order of the day. Receiving candid input from your advisers, the people who know you, and your family, are vital for your growth. Support and the willingness to learn are the two factors that will take you far in your quest to master leadership skills.

> **Keep your ear to the ground and listen to the winds of change.**

Embrace the future! Keep your ear to the ground and listen to the winds of change. Be aware of what's coming and what's shifting so you can be proactive and make smart decisions instead of being surprised by the inevitable changes of life.

CONTINUOUS EDUCATION

Changes in technology result in changes to every career field. A continuing commitment to learn and implement new ideas is vital. If you find yourself falling behind (and there are a variety of reasons that might cause that to happen), convince yourself to get back on track and recommit yourself to learning new things. Remember that no one is perfect, not even leaders, so if something happens that causes you to fall behind, just pick up where you left off and continue on. Failure to keep up with current business, social, and technological changes is directly linked to failure. The better-educated individual is the one who'll stand the best chance of achieving success in his or her career.

Knowledge is power, and is the result of education and training. Your ability to apply your knowledge influences your earning power. An electrician, for example, who's never taken training classes can't contribute very much to an organization; nor can they capitalize on opportunities. Be humble. Learning doesn't stop when you achieve your goal of completing your apprenticeship. At the very least you'll need to learn of changes to the National Electrical Code® every three years in order to stay current in your field.

Whether you're on the job, or in a social environment, there's something new you can learn. Embrace every opportunity to increase your knowledge of your trade or enhance your skills so you can increase your productivity, and then qualify for advancement. Take a course at least once a year in something that will improve your leadership skills. Compare what you've done with the goals that you've set. Ask yourself, "What technical or personal skills or certifications have I acquired lately?" If you don't have the latest skills and don't let your employer, supervisor, or potential employers know, then you're robbing yourself of the ability to truly be successful.

> **Knowledge is power, and is the result of education and training.**

If we never read a book on business or personal development, where can we expect to be years from now? How can we expect to grow? Leaders actively participate in life-long learning, even if it's simply a matter of reading ten pages of a good book each day. But, there's more information out there than any one person can keep up with. A lot of it will provide us with the knowledge we need to perform effectively. To better manage the time you spend reading without losing out on vital information, learn to read efficiently; skim the table of contents and directories, gloss over the headlines, find what's pertinent to you, and then spend time reading that material in depth. You can always go back and fill in the details when you have time. Learn to read more quickly by taking a speed-reading course.

Section 5 | Staying on Top of Your Game

Are you one of those people who have a mountain of letters, notes, magazines, and books waiting for you to sort through and read? It may look hopeless and the first thought many of us have is to just throw it all out—it takes less time and will certainly eliminate the "mountain." If you're about to tackle that mountain (or are trying to avoid it altogether), here are a few helpful suggestions to better manage what you read:

- Develop a list of books, magazines, and newspapers that you want to read, and read them first. Set goals and reasons for reading each source of information. Establish a year-long reading plan, and then follow through. Read with a purpose.

- Eliminate everything you really don't need to read. This not only helps to save time, but it makes the piles look smaller, which is encouraging.

> **Eliminate everything you really don't need to read.**

- Cancel subscriptions to magazines you don't read or need—it saves you money and time. Get off mailing lists for information that's not necessary or enjoyable for you to read. Yes, enjoyable! Be sure to take some time in your day to relax and pursue your own interests.

- Keep a constant check of what you read and evaluate its importance to you. If you don't need it, throw it away.

- Put deadlines on your reading materials. If you haven't read those magazines in over two months, you probably never will—throw them out!

- Keep a file folder of articles you want to re-read or refer to. Just tear out what you need, rather than keeping the entire magazine. Learn to skim over these and circle the ideas you find important and want to remember.

- Take your reading on the road. Set up a reading folder that's portable so you can read prior to appointments, or while waiting in a doctor's office. Better yet, catch up by reading your books and magazines on your tablet or phone.

- If there's information on a topic that you need, go to the web. Search for that topic and read what you need to know online without purchasing and storing unnecessary publications.

- If there's a particular topic you'd like to be informed about, set up a Google Alert for your email account. You can enter a subject or topic on which you want to be current, and every day you'll get an automatically generated email with a list of all relevant articles. Read those that interest you, and then delete them.

Take advantage of technology. Put your books, work, spreadsheets and reports on your laptop, tablet or smartphone, and sync them, so that when you read something or take action on something, the results are reflected on all your devices. Having your reading resources portable makes it easier for you to access them, get through them, or archive them. Sometimes we can go overboard with new technology, and it actually hampers our progress. There's a lot of research that shows we retain much more of what we read and study when we're holding the actual paper in our hands as opposed to looking at a screen. Some of us might conduct our business on computers but prefer our educational reading to be on printed media.

> Learning how to ask questions is one of the most powerful tools a leader can have.

Learning how to ask questions is one of the most powerful tools a leader can have. Find a mentor, ask lots of questions, and make a commitment to learn as much as you can from them. Talk to colleagues, employees, and customers frequently to learn information about your business, and find out what's really going on in the process so you'll be ready for future changes.

Learning and training should never end. Reading, continuing education, and seminars are all important if you truly wish to be a successful leader. You must keep up to the best of your ability, even if it means setting aside an hour or two a week to browse the internet for new developments in your field. Failure to keep up has been directly linked to the failure of many people.

Your time is limited. Make every moment count!

MEMBERSHIPS

Many industries have associations that are run and attended by individuals actively engaged in doing business in that field. They typically schedule meetings, trade shows, develop standards, and produce many worthwhile publications. These are prime sources of information about current and future trends relating to your chosen career. You'll develop a great network of people by becoming active in various business and social organizations. You'll enhance your own professional reputation, increase your knowledge, and open up pathways to future successes and opportunities.

Consider becoming a member of organizations that relate to your position. You can start by attending meetings, then volunteering to work on a committee or even head one up. This provides opportunities where you can demonstrate your initiative, cooperative spirit, and leadership qualities. Once you've been involved, you can add that to your resume. You'll also build a whole set of new contacts who'll remember your hard work and dedication. Don't throw that away! Remember that your self-branding, your image, includes those with whom you associate.

Social media sites are a way to stay connected and at the same time grow your professional image. Get involved and become aware of best practices on Facebook, Google Plus, LinkedIn and others, and always be aware of what you post and how it can be perceived—stay professional.

Although memberships can greatly enhance your connections, knowledge and exposure be careful that you don't let association memberships and attendance take more time than you can afford—either professionally or personally. The rewards of participation should be enough to warrant your continued attendance. If you find that it's causing a problem, reevaluate your association memberships and select those which provide you with the most benefit. Remember that you must always manage your time in a way that enhances your productivity and leadership skills. Never allow external commitments to control your schedule to the detriment of your career or your equally vital private life.

> **Memberships can greatly enhance your connections, knowledge, and exposure.**

PROCRASTINATION

Avoid Procrastination. It's something all of us do, but hopefully only occasionally. Think about yourself for a moment. When something needs to be done, do you step up to the plate and do it even though you don't want to, or do you put it off until "tomorrow?" If you're one of those people who put things off (procrastinate), you need to make a change. Many times the hardest part of completing a task is simply getting started. Make a commitment now to spend at least 15 minutes every day doing something that needs to be done in your work life or personal life. Set aside that minimum of 15 minutes early in the day even if it means getting up 15 minutes earlier in the morning. You might be surprised about how much better you feel as you complete the tasks you've been putting off.

> **Habitual procrastination is a problem with huge consequences, health being just one of them.**

Habitual procrastination is a problem with huge consequences, health being just one of them; so let's do some problem solving. People procrastinate for a variety of reasons. If you identify those reasons and deal with them directly and realistically it won't be a problem anymore. Some of the reasons for procrastination are:

- **Perfectionism**. Some people have impossibly high standards. In this situation, they're likely to put off doing something that they fear can't be accomplished perfectly. Think performance, instead of absolute perfection. Set manageable, concrete, incremental goals to be accomplished at specified times.

- **Large Overwhelming Tasks**. If a task seems so large and complex you don't know where to begin, you'll often put off getting started. If you don't start, you won't finish! In a situation like this, break the project into manageable units that will take you no more than ten to thirty minutes to complete. Take one small step at a time and build on your successes.

- **Unpleasant Tasks**. If you hate doing something, you're very likely to put off addressing it. When possible, delegate or hire someone to do the tasks that you dread the most. If you must do them yourself, think about how good you'll feel when the job you've been avoiding is done. Do unpleasant tasks first to get them out of the way and free up the rest of your day to pursue more pleasant activities.

- **Creating Pressure to Perform**. Some people motivate themselves by creating the pressure of a crisis atmosphere. They procrastinate until the last minute and then dramatically complete the work. Even though this strategy actually helps them get the task done, they're often confirmed procrastinators. The emotional expense, however, is great and detracts from the kind of consistent, concentrated effort a successful leader needs. So instead, motivate yourself by working at a reasonable pace to finish one step at a time rather than working yourself into a panic then doing it all in one last-ditch effort.

Some of the ways to reduce procrastination are to:

- Break the task into small manageable pieces.
- Do the hardest part first.
- Don't worry about being perfect.
- Give yourself a deadline.
- Reward yourself when you complete the task.
- Set a fixed time to work on the project.

> Sometimes procrastination is a warning signal.

Sometimes procrastination is a warning signal, a way to tell you that this isn't the right thing to do or that it's a waste of time and doesn't need doing. When, for whatever reason, you find that you continue to avoid important tasks, identify what you're doing instead, and cut off your escape routes. If you chronically procrastinate and find you just can't get started, ask yourself the following questions:

- **Under What Circumstances Will I be Motivated to do What Needs to be Done?** Listen carefully to your answer. Don't try to modify it. Think about what's stopping you from doing what you need to do. If you're honest with yourself, you might recognize you're not willing to work as long or hard as it takes to get the job done. Maybe you didn't schedule enough free time for yourself. Perhaps you aren't willing to do some of the tasks your work entails. In any case, now you have to face the truth because you're the leader. If you're unable to solve your own problems and to manage yourself, what will your future hold?

- **Do I Enjoy my Work?** If the honest answer is "no," then it's no wonder you're having difficulty getting yourself to do the tasks involved. If you really don't like your work, seriously consider finding something different, whether it's asking your employer to rearrange your responsibilities or leaving to work in another field.

There are many resources that address procrastination and how to over come it. Brian Tracy's *Eat That Frog!* is just one of them.

STRESS MANAGEMENT

"Stress" can be defined simply as the way you react physically and emotionally to change. Like change, stress can be either positive or negative. It might be the sense of anxiety you feel when faced with a new and challenging situation, or perhaps the vague sense of anxiety you feel after "one of those days!" In any case, you can learn to manage stress rather than allowing it to manage you.

Your stress response is automatic, like blinking your eyes. When faced with a challenging situation, your muscles tense, your heart rate and blood pressure increase, you might perspire more, and you might even notice a gripping sensation in your stomach. It's possible you'll also feel more mentally alert and focused. This stress response prepares your body to meet an immediate, recognizable challenge.

Stress can be caused by a sense of frustration and/or anxiety—trying to do too many things yourself. It occurs when you run out of time and must carry tasks over from one day to the next. This is followed by knowing that the "to-do's" that are carried over to the next day will be added to a whole new list of "things to do." You then start feeling boxed in with no escape and no alternatives. To minimize stress—handle what you can, delegate what you can't, and say "no" when necessary!

> In its positive aspect, stress can help you concentrate, focus, and perform.

Positive Stress. When stress is positive, your body automatically relaxes after you've handled the situation that triggered your stress response. Your muscles relax and your heart rate, blood pressure, and other physical functions all return to their normal, pre-stressed state. This relaxation response is the most important aspect of positive stress because it allows you to rest and gather the physical and emotional energy you need to meet the next challenge. Positive stress is a series of heightened alert and relaxation responses that help you deal with the changes and challenges of daily life.

In its positive aspect, stress can help you concentrate, focus, perform, and can often help you reach your peak efficiency. Many people, in fact, do their best work when under pressure. Then, when the challenge has been met, they take the time to relax and enjoy their achievements. This relaxation response allows them to build up the physical and emotional reserves to meet the next challenge, and is one of the key elements of positive stress.

Negative Stress. With negative stress, there's no true relaxation between one stress "crisis" and the next. When your body remains geared up, physical and emotional strain can result. Left uncontrolled, negative stress can lead to high blood pressure, ulcers, migraines, heart attacks—and worse. Fortunately, you can stop the cycle of negative stress by becoming aware of your stress and how you react to it by practicing relaxation techniques, and by developing a positive attitude and lifestyle.

Section 5 | Staying on Top of Your Game

Stress becomes negative when you stay "geared-up" and don't (or can't) relax after meeting the challenge. In today's world, where many situations can "push our buttons," it's no wonder we can't relax. For some people, stress becomes a way of life. Unfortunately, when it becomes a constant, ongoing cycle, your health and well-being will suffer. The good news is that with proper management, it need not be hazardous to your health. Understand, too, that your stress level not only affects you, but also those around you who love and care about you.

Managing Stress

Awareness. In order to manage stress, it's helpful to know what causes it and how you feel when you're under stress. Try to identify the situations in your life that make you feel tense. Then, "listen" to your body for signs such as headaches, stomach upsets, tensed muscles, clenched teeth, and cold or clammy hands which are stress indicators.

Relaxation Techniques. As you know, stress can be positive when it's balanced with relaxation. However, when it's constant and unrelieved, it can become a negative and even a destructive force. You can break the cycle of negative stress by learning ways to help yourself relax. By taking the time to practice simple relaxation techniques on a regular basis, you can give yourself a chance to unwind and prepare for life's next challenge.

> A positive attitude and lifestyle are key elements to managing your stress.

Positive Attitude and Lifestyle. A positive attitude and lifestyle are key elements to managing your stress. Since it's both an emotional and physical reaction to change, the better you feel (in body and mind), the better you'll be able to deal with the everyday stress in your life. When you learn to think positively, exercise, eat well, and rest regularly, you'll be taking care of the most important person you know—you!

Developing a Positive Attitude

- **Self-talk** means telling yourself what you can or can't do. Positive self-talk is saying "I can," and setting your mind to meet the challenge at hand.

- **Rehearsal** is a way to prepare for a potentially stressful situation before it occurs. Think about the situation, go over the details, plan the action to take, and visualize proceeding successfully.

- **Developing an action plan** can help you turn a stress disaster into a new opportunity. Always make an alternate plan, just in case the one you rehearsed doesn't work out.

Developing a Positive Lifestyle

- **Exercise.** Physically fit people handle stress more easily than those who aren't since they're apt to feel better about themselves in general. A regular exercise program should include some form of aerobic activity. Aerobic exercise helps your body use oxygen more efficiently and strengthens your heart and lungs. Running, walking, swimming, and bicycling are all excellent aerobic activities. Stretching exercises are also helpful in relieving tense muscles and improving overall flexibility. Exercise will actually reduce the negative effects of stress on your body because it releases the energy that's created by your stress response.

- **Nutrition.** When planning your meals, remember that the old saying, "You are what you eat!" is true—junk foods and refined sugars are low in nutritional value and generally high in calories. Food is your body's fuel—so give it "high test!" Plan your meals around servings from the four basic food groups: proteins, dairy products, grains, and fresh fruits and vegetables. Eating well, and limiting your use of salt, sugar, caffeine, and alcohol can promote health and help reduce stress.

- **Rest and Relaxation.** You already realize that relaxation is a key to balancing stress, but in addition to specific techniques, try to "slow down" and enjoy your leisure time. Realize that sometimes the best thing you can do for yourself is nothing at all. Don't cram your days full of endless chores—make an effort to relax and enjoy your free time. And, try to get to bed at a reasonable hour, especially if you're under stress. Your body needs sleep to refresh itself, and you need sleep to feel refreshed.

> Proper planning and goal setting gives you a sense of stability during the workday.

Proper planning and goal setting gives you a sense of stability during the workday. Delegation alleviates some of the responsibility you're carrying. Encourage those in your life to bring solutions—not problems! And, take time out for personal pursuits with the family, at meetings, hobbies, and so on. If you can't control the situations that create stress for you, then learn to control your reaction to them.

Conclusion

There's a lot of effort involved in staying on top of your game and remaining competitive, and now seems the right time to bring your attention to a very important tenet that will emphasize the importance of what we've discussed.

The Peter Principle is a concept in management theory introduced by Canadian sociologist Laurence J. Peter in his humoristic book of the same title. He claims that the selection of a candidate for a position is based on the candidate's performance in their current role, rather than on abilities relevant to the intended role. Thus, employees only stop being promoted once they can no longer perform effectively, and "managers rise to the level of their incompetence."

Don't let this be you. The problem isn't with a promotion, but rather with the lack of education and training to prepare for new duties. Know what you're good at, and focus on becoming great. Learn your trade and enhance your skills; first increase your productivity and then qualify for advancement.

The same holds true for those who you're leading and training. Remember that you can never know the circumstances other people around you are in, what they were born with, or what they had to overcome. What's more important, achievement or effort? The answer is effort. It's not important where you are on the ladder, but the direction in which you're going.

FINAL THOUGHTS

SUMMARY OF LEADERSHIP CHARACTERISTICS

I leave you with this summary of some key characteristics we consider defining for an effective leader. Use it as a checklist for how you feel about your current skills and which of those you feel need to be improved. It's a great bird's-eye view of what your journey will entail. For this journey to be a successful one, it has to be built on your passions and desires.

BE as Many of the Following as Possible:

1. **Trusting.** It's essential for you to be able to trust those you're leading (supervising, directing, and so on). This trust needs to be balanced with a willingness to identify people who've proven they can't be trusted to make some tough decisions and remove them, or minimize their negative impact on the goal(s) of the group. Without trust and mutual respect among leaders and followers (subordinates), a group (organization) will often suffer from a combination of low performance and poor morale.

2. **Visible and Approachable.** Some organizations find the application of the four-hour rule a useful guideline. This guideline recommends that leaders should spend no more than four hours a day in their offices. The rest of the time, they should be out with their people. They should be talking with people engaged in production, and with customers to directly obtain their recommendations and comments on problem areas. They should be patting people on the back, making short informal speeches, and handing out awards. They should be traveling widely throughout their spheres of influence, and they should be making contact with other key organizations and influencing personnel to ensure that relationships are enhanced and problem areas identified early.

3. **Decisive—But Patiently Decisive.** Leaders should listen to all sides before making a decision. A decisive leader is an effective leader; an impulsive leader is rarely effective. However, postponing a decision for many weeks or months is rarely a productive tactic. A non-decision is in itself a decision and should be recognized as such. Risk-taking is frequently an unavoidable essential and healthy aspect of decision-making. Leaders should understand how to implement decisions. They must ensure that decisions aren't only carried out but also carried out faithfully in both substance and spirit. While agreement isn't always obtainable, acceptance and willing compliance are a must.

4. **Introspective.** Leaders should be able to look at themselves objectively and analyze where they've made mistakes, where they've turned people off, and where they've headed down the wrong path.

Final Thoughts

5. **Reliable.** Reliability is something leaders must have in order to provide stability and strength to the group. Be careful about what commitments are made, but once those commitments are firm, nothing should stop you from honoring them unless they're renegotiated. Important elements of reliability are persistence and consistency. Leaders must be willing to be flexible, but consistency and persistence are important elements of positive leadership.

6. **Principled.** Work ethics are the principals by which you conduct yourself on the job. Leaders shouldn't just talk about integrity, they must practice it. Integrity shouldn't lie dormant until a crisis occurs; it must be ingrained and nurtured by the entire group. Of all the qualities a leader must have, integrity is the most important.

7. **Open-minded.** The best leaders are those whose minds are never closed and who are eager to view issues from the vantage point or the perspective of others. Leaders shouldn't frequently change their minds after a major decision has been made, but if they never do so, they're beginning to show a degree of rigidity and inflexibility that can spell trouble for the group.

8. **Dignified.** When standards of dignity are established and routinely emphasized, everyone can take pride in both the accomplishments and the stylistic image of the group. A happy combination of substance and style leads to high performance and morale.

9. **Healthy and Fit.** The demands of leadership are very heavy, and no matter how well you might plan your schedule, there'll be times when the pressures and demands will be oppressive. A physical fitness program can help you be prepared for those difficult periods that occur in leadership roles.

10. **Technically Savvy.** Leaders must not only understand the major elements of the group with which they're involved, they must also keep up with changes. If a leader has a high level of technical competence, then they should be able to trust their intuition. This combination of competence and intuition can be an extremely powerful tool.

DO as Much of the Following as You Can:

1. **Share.** Teaching and leadership go hand-in-hand. A leader must be willing to teach skills, to share insights and experiences, and to work very closely with people to help them mature and be creative. In order to be a good teacher, you must be a good communicator.

2. **Problem-Solve.** While it's important for a leader be a problem solver, he or she should also facilitate problem solving skills in others by encouraging them to participate in the process. Give them the opportunity to bring you the solution rather than the problem. The reward that a follower (employee/subordinate) receives from actually solving

problems is important. It builds self-esteem and enhances their ability to do even better in subsequent situations. By being the problem solver of last resort, a leader can help the group grow and thrive.

3. **Manage Time Effectively.** One of the great faults many people have is the general failure to discipline their schedules; in-boxes, telephones, continuing education, meetings, leisure time, the demands of your family, and on and on. Staying busy and working very long hours don't equate to leadership effectiveness. On the other hand, becoming and remaining organized frees up your time by giving you the ability to work more efficiently.

4. **Set High Standards.** Leaders must be willing to set high standards, abide by them unwaveringly, and encourage their followers to live by those same high standards. Employees who are unable to adhere to them after training drain the organization and its capable leaders of the time, energy, and attention needed to accomplish their mission. In a business setting with circumstances such as these, leaders have a responsibility to the organization to remove those who stand in the way of success. When it's necessary to remove people from key positions, leaders should meet with those individuals personally. The removal should be done with grace, style, and firmness. When you call individuals in to ask them to move on, you should be willing to do so—and not end the meeting until you get to the point. In our highly legalistic society, you must know and abide by the laws relating to employee discharge.

5. **Take Care of Your People.** Leaders should recognize not just the top performers but also the many others who are doing their jobs well. They should *never* ask employees (or followers) to write their own personal evaluations or effectiveness report(s). Leaders should write them and make sure they're done with care and style. Leaders should recognize outstanding followers (employees/subordinates), while avoiding the pitfalls of favoritism. Thanking people is an important part of taking care of them, because it's taking care of their psychological health.

6. **Plan Strategically.** Leaders may run an efficient and effective group or organization, but they don't really serve long-term interests unless they plan, set goals, and provide strategic vision. Those leaders who aren't visionaries (and many aren't) should ensure they have frequent contact with people who have a talent and an inclination for long-range planning, visionary thinking, and innovation. The best leaders are agents for change, and one of the best ways to ensure change is accomplished systematically through good long-range planning.

7. **Put Personal Ambitions Aside.** Leaders must often subvert their own ambitions in order to ensure the development and maturation of those they lead. If leaders are too ambitious for the organization, or too ambitious for themselves, they may drive the organization in dysfunctional directions. They become a part of the problem rather than a part of the solution.

Final Thoughts

8. **Run Effective Meetings.** Much of a leader's time is spent in meetings of one sort or another. Leaders should know what kind of meetings they're attending; they should establish the ground rules for them; and they should be actively involved to make sure they stay on track while allowing individuals ample opportunity to express their views and their disagreements. Finally, leaders should know how to wrap meetings up, to draw conclusions, to set up the time and agenda for the next one on the subject, and to direct individuals in attendance to carry out certain tasks as a result of the decisions that have been made. Leaders must also discontinue routine meetings that aren't serving an important purpose. Meetings should serve to accomplish a specific goal. It's important to have, and use, written agendas; those who don't are too easily misdirected.

9. **Motivate.** Leaders can't individually reach all of their people on a regular basis, so they must count on others to provide needed motivation. Commitment to mission, love of the job and the people, dedication to high standards, frequent reinforcement of the organization's plans and goals, strong incentives rewards, and lots of compliments for hard work and high performance are all parts of the vital motivation factor.

10. **Have a Sense of Humor.** Leaders should let people know that everyday life (professional or personal) isn't so formal and intense that you can't sit back occasionally and be amused by what's happening. Humor can be a great tension reliever. Be relaxed and be humorous with people in a positive manner. Negative humor delivered with an acid tongue, intended to belittle others, is unprofessional and counterproductive. Off-color humor should be avoided, since it diminishes the dignity of you and everyone around you.

This list might appear to be daunting at first, but no-one said it was going to be simple! Don't think of key characteristics as a list of requirements in order to be a leader—think of them as a work in progress. They're skills that you'll acquire and perfect as you gain knowledge, experience, and confidence. Just make a commitment to be 100 percent responsible for yourself, to learn everything you can about your job, and do it the best that you possibly can. Just do some of the things that leaders do and you'll be surprised—the sky's the limit. Just by having read this material, you're well on your way.

BALANCE (LIFE)—ALL THINGS IN PROPORTION

One of the biggest dangers you face as you develop your career is allowing your work or studies to overshadow all other areas of your life. Remember that your goal to become a leader is to build a good life for yourself and your family—all in the pursuit of happiness. It's self-defeating if you're achieving your written goals, or have achieved them, and make yourself miserable in the process.

Don't neglect outside activities that are necessary in order for you to enjoy a balanced life. Your career certainly demands your attention for long-range planning and success, but you need to schedule time for friends and family activities—after all they're your best support. Take an active part in social affairs, religious worship, and hobbies. Select activities that develop not only your body but also your views and your mind as well.

Wherever you might be on your path to becoming a leader, incorporating the topics we've discussed into your daily life should result in success. You might have already mastered some of them, some you might have heard of but think you can't do, and some will be completely new concepts to you. The truth is that everyone can master these skills—it may take some time and a little bit of work, but the results are worth the effort.

Remember to apply the things you've learned here to all aspects of your life, not just to your career. Apply them to yourself, your relationships, and your spiritual growth too. Without a good balance between professional time and personal time, you won't be able to develop the effective personal and leadership skills that are vital to your success.

True success is knowing what a great life looks like for you, and then developing your skills and yourself while keeping focused on why you're doing this in the first place.

Notes